Trafficked Young People

Human trafficking constitutes one of the most serious human rights violations of our time. However, many social work practitioners still have a poor and incomplete understanding of the experiences of children and young people who have been trafficked. In *Trafficked Young People*, the authors call for a more sophisticated, informed and better-developed understanding of the range of issues facing trafficked young people.

In the first work of its kind to combine an up-to-date overview of the current policy context with related theoretical concerns and practitioner experiences, Pearce, Hynes and Bovarnick demonstrate how the trafficking of children and young people should be regarded as a child protection, rather than an immigration concern. Drawing on focus group and interview research with 72 practitioners and covering the cases of 37 individuals, *Trafficked Young People* explores the way child care practitioners identify, understand and work with the problems faced by people who have been trafficked. The book looks at how practitioners interpret and use definitions of trafficking in their day-to-day work, at their experiences of exposing the needs of trafficked children and young people, and at their efforts to find appropriate resources to meet these needs.

Trafficked Young People will be of interest to practitioners working with children in social work, youth justice, education and health contexts. With its emphasis on the legal and policy framework, and integrated throughout with case histories, practitioner interviews and recommendations for best practice, *Trafficked Young People* is essential reading for anyone working within a social policy development context.

Jenny J. Pearce is the Director of the Institute of Applied Social Research, and the International Centre for the Study of Sexually Exploited and Trafficked Young People, both at the University of Bedfordshire, UK. Her research interests focus particularly on young people, sexual exploitation, child protection and domestic violence, and on accessing young people's accounts of their experiences of child sexual exploitation.

Patricia Hynes is a Principal Lecturer in the Department of Applied Social Studies at the University of ... s include the sociology of human rights and ... ng trafficking, refugees and issues around ... nationally on internally displaced persons.

D1145782

Silvie Bovarnick is a freelance researcher. She has previously worked for the NSPCC and the Department of Health on research programmes addressing different areas of violence and abuse. Her academic interests include the discursive construction of human rights and violence, specifically covering children's rights and women's rights. She has recently conducted research on child trafficking and child neglect.

Adolescence and Society
Series Editor: John C. Coleman
Department of Education, University of Oxford

In the 20 years since it began, this series has published some of the key texts in the field of adolescent studies. The series has covered a very wide range of subjects, almost all of them being of central concern to students, researchers and practitioners. A mark of its success is that a number of books have gone to second and third editions, illustrating its popularity and reputation.

The primary aim of the series is to make accessible to the widest possible readership important and topical evidence relating to adolescent development. Much of this material is published in relatively inaccessible professional journals, and the objective of the books has been to summarise, review and place in context current work in the field, so as to interest and engage both an undergraduate and a professional audience.

The intention of the authors is to raise the profile of adolescent studies among professionals and in institutions of higher education. By publishing relatively short, readable books on topics of current interest to do with youth and society, the series makes people more aware of the relevance of the subject of adolescence to a wide range of social concerns.

The books do not put forward any one theoretical viewpoint. The authors outline the most prominent theories in the field and include a balanced and critical assessment of each of these. Whilst some of the books may have a clinical or applied slant, the majority concentrate on normal development.

The readership rests primarily in two major areas: the undergraduate market, particularly in the fields of psychology, sociology and education; and the professional training market, with particular emphasis on social work, clinical and educational psychology, counselling, youth work, nursing and teacher training.

Also in this series:

Illegal Leisure Revisited
Judith Aldridge, Fiona Measham and Lisa Williams

The Nature of Adolescence, 4th Edition
John C. Coleman

Wired Youth
Gustavo Mesch and Ilan Talmud

Moving Out, Moving On
Shelley Mallett, Doreen Rosenthal, Deb Keys and Roger Averill

Adolescent Coping
Erica Frydenberg

Social Networks in Youth and Adolescence
John Cotterell

Growing Up with Unemployment
Anthony H. Winefield

Sexuality in Adolescence
Susan M. Moore and Doreen A. Rosenthal

Identity in Adolescence
Jane Kroger

Young People's Leisure and Lifestyles
Anthony Glendenning, Leo Hendry, John Love and Janet Shucksmith

Illegal Leisure
Judith Aldridge, Fiona Measham and Howard Parker

Personality Development in Adolescence
Eva Skoe and Anna von der Lippe

Smoking in Adolescence
Barbara Lloyd, and Kevin Lucas

Young People's Involvement in Sport
John Kremer, Shaun Ogle and Karen Trew

Youth, AIDS and Sexually Transmitted Diseases
Anne Mitchell, Susan Moore and Doreen Rosenthal

Adolescent Health
Patrick Heave

Teenagers and Technology
Chris Davies and Rebecca Eynon

Trafficked Young People

Breaking the wall of silence

Jenny J. Pearce, Patricia Hynes and Silvie Bovarnick

Routledge
Taylor & Francis Group

LONDON AND NEW YORK

First published 2013
by Routledge
27 Church Road, Hove, East Sussex BN3 2FA

Simultaneously published in the USA and Canada
by Routledge
711 Third Avenue, New York, NY 10017

Routledge is an imprint of the Taylor & Francis Group, an informa business

British Library Cataloguing in Publication Data
A catalogue record for this book is available from the British Library

Library of Congress Cataloging-in-Publication Data
Pearce, Jenny J. Trafficked young people :
breaking the wall of silence / Jenny Pearce,
Patricia Hynes & Silvie Bovarnick.
p. cm.
1. Child trafficking—Great Britain.
2. Child abuse—Great Britain.
3. Abused children—Services for—Great Britain.
I. Hynes, Patricia. II. Bovarnick, Silvie. III. Title
HQ281.P425 2012
362.760941—dc23
2012026376

ISBN: 978–0–415–61751–2 (hbk)
ISBN: 978–0–415–61754–3 (pbk)
ISBN: 978–0–203–07494–7 (ebk)

Typeset in Times New Roman
by Swales & Willis Ltd, Exeter, Devon

Printed and bound in Great Britain by
TJ International Ltd, Padstow, Cornwall

Contents

Acknowledgements

We would like to thank the University of Bedfordshire and The Children's Charity and the NSPCC for their financial support to enable the research informing this book to take place. Professor Susanne MacGregor was chair of the research advisory group and in that role provided a professional, objective, informed and stimulating lead to the work. Her support was, and always has been, invaluable. Nadine Finch provided guidance and expertise on the legislative context to the work as it was taking place and as we continued to write. We are extremely grateful to her. The NSPCC's Child Trafficking Advice and Information Line(CTAIL) project, ECPAT UK(End Child Prostitution, Child Pornography and Trafficking of Children for Sexual Purposes UK) and the Refugee Council all provided expert advice on particular aspects of the trafficking of young people. Their work continues to raise awareness about and guide current initiatives to challenge trafficking and to support trafficked young people. The research project that provided data for this work and the continuing development of initiatives from it have been administered and organised by Cara Senouni. Her professional, calm and efficient ways of ensuring smooth project management have impressed everyone who ever comes into contact with her.

Mandy John Baptiste and her colleagues at the NSPCC CTAIL provided an essential reference point for consultation on current policy and practice pertaining to the trafficking of young people. The CTAIL Young People's Advisory Group provided invaluable support by commenting on draft case study templates and advising on the content and delivery of the research. Their bravery in managing their own circumstances while providing considered support to the research was exemplary.

We would also like to thank the practitioners, agencies and local authorities that participated in our research for giving their time and sharing their expertise. Their insight into the realities of working with trafficked children made this project possible and meaningful.

In particular we would like to thank our families and friends for supporting us while we completed this research, and then throughout the process of writing the book. Mark Powell and Robbie Oates, Anne Marie and Rosie Burr, and Aaron Bovarnick have given time and support throughout. Finally, we thank the Series Editor, John Coleman, for essential advice and guidance and for supporting and encouraging us to ensure that this book came to fruition.

1 Introduction

This book looks at the trafficking of young people into, within and out of the UK. It focuses on the responses of child care practitioners to trafficked young people in the UK, looking at what they understand trafficking to be and how they describe the complexities in their work with trafficked young people. It draws on research carried out by the authors between 2007 and 2009. Funded by the National Society for the Prevention of Cruelty to Children (NSPCC) and the University of Bedfordshire, the research held focus groups and interviews with a total of 72 practitioners and studied 37 cases of trafficked young people.

Before looking at the findings from the research, we introduce in this chapter some of the conceptual and legislative frameworks and the policy contexts in which the trafficking of children has been placed. We look at the key issues that will figure throughout the book, introducing the central themes that emerged from our research: that the trafficking of young people includes international trafficking across borders and 'internal' domestic trafficking within the UK; that the trafficking of young people is a child protection issue; and that concerns have focused on young women trafficked for sexual exploitation at the expense of encompassing all forms of abuse of both young women and young men. Leading on from this, it is recognised that the impact of abuse can best be addressed through the creation of supportive relationships with caring, trained and experienced staff who, through engaging well with the young person, can 'model' a good relationship, providing an alternative for the young person to the abusive experiences hitherto known. This chapter then engages with a critical appraisal of 'risk' and 'resilience', and what is meant by an age assessment, addressing why understanding this is so important when working with trafficked young people. Finally, an outline is given of the key points explored in subsequent chapters of the book.

The context for human trafficking: protecting young people from abuse

Human trafficking, and in particular the trafficking of children and young people, constitutes one of the most serious human rights violations of our time. International inequalities are exploited, with force, coercion and deception leading to abuses of power that can, if they are not identified, harm young people for the rest of their lives. In a world where the control of migration is the aim of many governments, the way nation-states govern entry has serious implications for all migrants, including children and young people who migrate (Dwyer *et al.* 2011; O'Connell Davidson and Farrow 2007). In this context, human trafficking is a hidden and clandestine activity.

Human trafficking is thought to be the third most profitable organised criminal activity in the world, after weapons and narcotics. Given the inherent difficulties in quantifying human trafficking in general, and child trafficking in particular, rigorous or reliable statistics that could lead to improvements to policy or practice remain elusive. The perception that human trafficking is orchestrated only by organised criminals, rather than opportunistic usage of social networks by ordinary people, is also problematic without clear proof.

Protecting children who have been trafficked is a complex endeavour. According to UNICEF, some 1.2 million children may be trafficked each year. The reference to children includes any child under the age of 18, as defined by the United Nations Convention on the Rights of the Child (UNCRC). In this book, we particularly focus on the trafficking of young people under the age of 18 in their adolescence, looking at the impact of trafficking on those in their teenage years. In doing so, we refer to the definition of the trafficked child as outlined in the Palermo Protocol of 2000, which notes the relationship between movement of the victim and the purpose of exploitation. The Protocol confirms that no child under the age of 18 can consent to being trafficked. Some of the limitations inherent in this definition are noted throughout this book, including potential tensions between delivering 'child-centred' approaches which recognise the agency of the child while regarding their welfare as of paramount importance (Children Act 1989), and 'immigration-centred' approaches which take border control as their central focus (Bovarnick 2010). As we note throughout the book, this is particularly pertinent for adolescents approaching adulthood, whose age may be disputed and for whom assumptions about capacity to cope may override their need for protection and support.

While the main focus of this book is on practitioners' responses to young people trafficked into the country from abroad, we are also mindful of young people's experience of continued trafficking within the UK. We also refer therefore to what is often termed 'internal trafficking' or 'domestic trafficking', including the continued movement within UK borders of young people trafficked from abroad, and the trafficking of young people born within the UK who are moved from area to area within the UK for the purpose of sexual exploitation (as outlined in the Sexual Offences Act 2003).

The trafficking of young people is child abuse

The central theme emerging from the research, and developed in the book, is that trafficking of children and young people is child abuse. Cases of trafficked young people who have had past experiences of war, poverty and abuse have raised questions about whether they should be seen as victims per se, or whether some, with the support and agreement of their families, are actively exercising some agency, putting themselves forward to be trafficked as a means of escaping adverse situations in their countries of origin. While questions of choice might be explored for adults who seek to leave their country of origin, the Palermo Protocol (2000), explained in more depth in chapter 2, defines children clearly as victims: 'Children under 18 cannot give valid consent, and any recruitment, transportation, transfer, harbouring or receipt of children for the purposes of exploitation is a form of trafficking regardless of the means used.'

As a result, and as is well documented from research elsewhere, trafficked young people should be supported through child protection procedures (Kelly and Bokhari 2011; Bokhari 2008; Home Office 2011; Pearce *et al.* 2009). They should not be subjected to undue questioning or interrogation about their journey into the UK, their age, or their immigration status (Crawley 2006). While it is important that child traffickers are prosecuted, evidence needed for conviction should follow from child protection interventions with the young people concerned, rather than precede the need to protect and secure the safety of the child. The need to believe the voice of the young person and to support them in disclosing details of their past experiences at their own pace, in their own time, in a place of security and safety is a central finding from our research. Recognising that interventions should respond to trafficked young people as 'victims' of abuse, we seek to provide evidence surrounding responses to the trafficking of young people in the UK while avoiding the view that a young person who has been trafficked will inevitably always remain a 'victim'. Developing through adolescence into adulthood, the young person will have opportunities to practise their own agency, to make decisions for their immediate and longer term future. The book explores some of the complexities identified by practitioners supporting young people who are making the transition from vulnerable 'victim' to independent autonomous agent.

The trafficking of young people for a range of forms of exploitation

A subsidiary theme emerging from the research and explored throughout the book is that although there is an increasing body of knowledge about trafficked children and young people, most is dominated by concern about trafficking for sexual exploitation, at the expense of awareness of other forms of exploitation (see also Jobe 2008, 2010). The recent political concern about the sexualisation of youth (Papadopoulos 2010), the dominant discourses of the 'sex slave trade' (see http://www.stopthetraffick.org) and the media's use of 'sex' in headlines to attract attention have all contributed to 'trafficking' being seen to mean trafficking for prostitution or for sexual exploitation. There is no doubt that young people are trafficked for sexual exploitation and that this is an abhorrent abuse of their rights which causes severe problems with physical, emotional, mental and sexual health. However, the trafficking of young people also takes place for other forms of exploitation, and many, such as domestic servitude and/or enforced criminality, often remain invisible to the general public (Kelly 2005). Although there has been some recent media concern about the trafficking of young people to work in cannabis factories, and coverage of the exploitation of Romany young people through forced labour, there is little empirical research that reveals the full extent of the variety of forms of exploitation; of the problems experienced by the young people concerned; or of the issues facing the range of practitioners trying to support them (Craig 2008; Dotteridge 2004; Garrett 2006). It was previously suggested by Salt (2000) that empirical evidence for trafficking is disproportionately small in comparison to the enormous interest and concern expressed by governmental and intergovernmental departments, non-governmental organisations (NGOs), the media and popular discourse. A decade later, little has changed, and there is still a need for further research to provide evidence to inform the development of knowledge and of appropriate service provision.

Relationship based thinking: modelling 'good' relationships

Finally, a further theme emerging from the research draws on the principles underpinning relationship based practice as proposed by Howe (1998) and suggested in Laming's (2009) and Monro's (2011) reports on social work practice (see also van de Glind 2010). This argues that social work interventions with children and young people need to draw on qualified, skilled and supported staff who can build meaningful and sustainable relationships with the young people they support. It is through building constructive and supportive relationships with trafficked young people that models of non-abusive, safe relationships can be grounded in the young person's experience, offering them a lived alternative to the abusive and neglectful relationships that may have, hitherto, become their norm. A secure relationship with a carer/practitioner instils confidence in the young person.

It is not enough for them to be given a handbook telling them of the services available, or to receive a one-off interview aimed at helping them to manage their circumstances, their finances and their access to education or training. This will not counter the deep mistrust and fear created by previous abusive experiences. Nor will it promote healing, which is an essential prerequisite of moving on. In order to rebuild their lives, young people need the opportunity to access professional help within a meaningful relationship to address past traumatic experiences. This takes time and requires trust to be built or rebuilt. The practitioner and/or carer needs to be able to engage in a 'good' relationship with the young person, helping them to feel secure and cared for. Then, and only then, will a confidence and security develop that will help them move on into independent and autonomous living.

These three themes underpin much of the discussion within the book:

- Trafficking of children is child abuse and young people should be worked with through child protection policies and procedures with the best interest of the child given paramount importance. This is in line with the requirement in the Children Act 1989 that the welfare of the child is of 'paramount' importance and with the UNCRC, which specifies basic human rights that children are entitled to receive.
- Young people can be trafficked for a range of different forms of abuse.
- Policies and procedures are not enough on their own: practitioners need to be able to model 'good' relationships with young people who have been trafficked, providing them with a safe environment within which they can (a) experience support and safety in their relationships with others, and (b) feel contained in a safe enough context to disclose their history of abuse.

Before moving to look at an outline of individual chapters in the book, there are two further broad considerations to be addressed, placing the experience of the trafficked young person in the context of questions of risk, resilience, childhood and transition through adolescence to adulthood. The first asks how our understanding of the relationship between risk, risk factors and resilience experienced by adolescents can inform our perceptions of the risks faced by a trafficked young person. The second asks what is already known about child protection interventions with the older age group of adolescents undergoing transition to adulthood.

Risk and resilience

Throughout the book we use terms such as 'victim' and 'at risk'. It is helpful to explore what we mean by these concepts in a little detail.

Young people may be 'at risk' of being trafficked because of environmental factors such as living in extreme poverty or living in war-torn areas or locations where there has been a natural disaster. Beyond the environmental risk factors, they may also be at risk of being trafficked because of family neglect, or because of individual risk factors such as low self-esteem or an inadequate education, meaning that they are poorly equipped to recognise or understand potential exploitation. Environmental risk factors (war or famine), familial risk factors (neglect and previous abuse) and individual risk factors (low self-esteem) can all compound each other to make the young person particularly vulnerable to, or 'at risk' of being trafficked.

On the other hand, young people who have been identified as trafficked are, because of their experiences, vulnerable to further risk of being isolated from mainstream services and of having poor emotional, sexual or mental health. That is, the experience of being trafficked can make the young person vulnerable to further harm. In addition, the trafficked young person may, because of experiences of abuse, or of forced, violent entry into informal economies, be seen as 'risky', demonstrating behaviours that are understood as presenting a risk to others or that challenge 'social norms'. Indeed, their behaviours may actually challenge the very interventions that are designed to support them.

These different 'typologies' of environmental, familial and individual risk factors, of different concepts of being 'at risk' and of presenting 'risky behaviours', have been well developed (Coleman and Hagel 2007; Coleman 2011; Luthar 2003). While explaining the typologies in more detail, this literature also develops informed critiques of an uncritical acceptance of the term 'risk'. It engages with a critique of the 'risk' society, arguing that a predominantly 'risk aware' society can create artificial attempts to measure and control environments and emotions that are fluid and changing (Beck 1992). When applied to practice, this is demonstrated in the proliferation of risk assessments which try to measure apparently static individual, familial and environmental factors. The work argues that not only can risk assessments be naive and false mechanisms designed to quantify the unquantifiable, but that 'labelling' a child as 'at risk' or 'vulnerable' may unhelpfully restrict a full comprehensive understanding of the child's potential to be an active agent in their own development (Cooper and Lousada 2005).

Following from this, it is recognised that 'risk' must be understood in relationship to 'resilience'. As research has identified typologies of risk, so too has it identified a range of forms of protective factors, all contributing to the young person's ability to build resilience, to manage and move on from harm. While there are individual, familial and environmental risk factors, so too there is a range of different protective factors operating at different levels that can help a young person to manage. These protective factors, identified as enhancing the young person's resilience, include individual factors such as intelligence and self-esteem; familial factors such as a supportive parent or carer; and environmental factors such as enabling education and empowering youth and community facilities. Awareness of the role of these protective factors in the development of resilience helps practitioners to engage with empowering the young person. For example, this means recognising the importance of interventions, including one-to-one support, ensuring safe and supportive accommodation and enabling access to school, youth and health service provisions.

One of the reoccurring themes that emerged from the research was the dominance of the focus on the victim, at the expense of awareness of attributing resilience to the young person. Although the research does show a reticence or inability on the part of practitioners to identify a trafficked young person, it is clear that once identified, the label 'victim', 'trafficked', 'vulnerable', 'at risk' or 'exploited' overshadowed other identities, leaving the young person feeling trapped within their circumstances, unable to move on. That is, the intervention was lead by a victim based 'deficit' model, seeing what the child did not have, the dangerous risks that they faced, rather than an 'asset' model, focusing more on protective factors that help them to build resilience. While the research showed the need for trafficked children to be worked with through child protection procedures as victims of abuse, it also noted the need for other aspects of the young person's development (education, health, recreation) to be acknowledged and respected.

In summary, the worry was that while child protection interventions took precedence, other service providers such as schools, youth and health services that could help the young person to build resilience took a 'back seat', being 'let off the hook' from having to reach out and ensure that services are accessible and meaningful.

Of course, meeting the needs of the whole child or young person is not simple, with the process being complicated by histories of abuse, neglect and violence. However, most young people want, and are capable of holding, multiple identities. They are a daughter or son, a part-time employee, a school student, a friend, a sports person, and/or an artist. This assertion, that identifiers are multiple, is developed well in literature about the social model of disability (Oliver 1990, and see Shakespeare and Watson 2002 for important developments on the social model of disability). This model illustrates the way a disabling environment, along with negative images of disablement in the media, compound the disabled person's experience as isolated and different, and limits scope for development of their various skills and multiple identities. Feminists make similar arguments with regard to the multiple identities of women, arguing that identities cannot be restricted to singular constructs such as 'race', 'gender', 'religion', 'age' or 'class', but that these are constantly changing and evolving and should be analysed in their interconnectedness and fluidity rather than as static and fixed signifiers. Although a young person may be defined as a 'victim' of trafficking, and therefore 'at risk' of associated harm, they may also be capable of being resilient, resourceful and inventive (Hynes 2010b). To limit the definition of 'self' to one identity such as 'a victim of trafficking' is to undermine the young person's attempt to be resilient, to progress into adulthood with multiple 'strings to their bow'.

Questions about a trafficked young person's status as 'victim' or active agent, or both, is further compounded by their own complex understanding of the role that they believe, or have been instructed to believe, they have played in their experience of being trafficked. The young person may have been told that it is their responsibility, that it is their fault that they are trafficked or that they owe the traffickers repayment for the costs of transport. The dynamics created here are explored further in chapter 5. For now, it is important to recognise that even in cases where the young person may be saying that they have chosen a particular course of action, they not be talking from an informed position, but rather from one of coercion and abuse. As stated in the UNCRC, all children under the age of 18 are entitled to protection from this form of abuse. It is recognised that intervening to support vulnerable young people in ways that also acknowledge and support the development of their own agency is complex (Melrose 2010). We develop this a little further below.

Child protection and adolescent transition to adulthood: when is a child not a child?

Although trafficked young people are defined as such for legal and child protection reasons, their experiences of abuse, violence and exploitation take place alongside the physical and psychological changes and developments occurring through adolescence. In this sense, they experience the same physical and psychological changes and developments as any teenager. The impact of trauma caused by being trafficked should not undermine our awareness of their needs as adolescents progressing through a particular stage of lifespan development.

It has long been argued that adolescents have been seen in a negative light: that rather than being perceived as young people able to make valuable contributions to family, community and society, 'teenagers' may often be seen as difficult and challenging (Coleman 2011; Hicks and Stein 2010). It is not unusual for child care service providers to note that adolescents are the hardest group to engage (Pearce 2009). Thus, Rees *et al.* (2010) argue that policy and practice that should be supporting neglected young people tend to overlook issues presented by vulnerable adolescents rather than giving serious consideration to how to engage and protect them.

Three different issues come to play here: service providers may not welcome young people, who may be feared or seen as too difficult to engage; young people themselves may feel hostile towards or alienated from services designed to support them; and, more specifically in relation to child protection, services may focus on safeguarding younger children perceived to be the most vulnerable, overlooking the needs of older adolescents.

Even before 2010 when the impact of the current government cuts started to be felt, the Directors of Children's Services noted that child protection focused on protecting younger children from abuse within the home. Invariably those older young people who were in need of support were demonised as 'trouble makers', as opposed to being seen as vulnerable and in need of support (Cook 2009). Indeed, the argument that 'safeguarding' focuses mainly on babies and that interventions to support teenagers are rarely preventative was suggested by Kim Bromley-Derry, chair of the Children's Interagency Group:

> Adolescents are a high risk group. There is a danger that we focus too much on the risk to babies and very young children . . . a number of services for young people, including youth offending services, tend to come into effect 'after the horse has bolted'.
>
> (Bromley-Derry in Cook 2009)

Similar arguments emerged from research undertaken by the Children's Society (Rees *et al.* 2010, noted above). Set against this backdrop, the current concern is that as UK child protection services are increasingly stretched, with local authority 'cutbacks' resulting in both an increase in child poverty and a simultaneous decrease in the breadth and depth of service provision available to support children in need, the scope of services to reach children other than the youngest, most vulnerable will diminish (Jago *et al.* 2011). As adolescents approach adulthood, a reduction in funding to support them can be justifiied on the grounds of their increasing autonomy, their increasing need for independence and the development of their own capacity to look after themselves, even against adversity. In a forthcoming publication, Pearce terms this professional abuse through 'condoned consent'. Condoned consent is where, either consciously or unconsciously, practitioners assume that the young person is in control of their actions, consenting to the abuse that they are experiencing. This condoned consent serves to act as a rationale for not intervening or allocating resources to support vulnerable teenagers.

Without undermining a young person's sense of agency, the evidence in this book argues that a trafficked teenager should not be seen to be responsible for the trauma and abuse they have experienced. The damage that can be caused, to both self-awareness, self-esteem, health and education are far from negligible and need a safeguarding, child protection response. The implications are that generic, universal services to young people should not emerge as 'too little, too late'. 'No action', even if some individuals or agencies may feel it to be a safer response than 'limited action', is unacceptable.

Since the death of Victoria Climbié in 2000 (Laming 2003) and baby Peter Connelly in 2007 (see Laming 2009), child protection has become a significant political and policy concern, with a renewed interest in social work practice (Munro 2011; Parton 2011). There is scope to build on this current interest and consider questions that arise for supporting trafficked young people. In short, these can be summarised as follows:

- When is a child not a child? Although it is clearly specified in the UNCRC that a child is anyone under the age of 18, asking this question engages us with questions about the social construction of the term. Recognising that 'childhood' may mean different things in different countries across the world helps us to question what we mean when we consider a child's transition to adulthood through adolescence. Some young people may be expected to fend for themselves, to work for money, to care for families and communities or to travel unaccompanied, while others are supported within secure environments protected from the impact of the economy or responsibilities as carers. Finally, serious questions are raised about how to proceed when the age of a trafficked child is disputed. Recent research into the well-being of unaccompanied asylum-seeking children (UASC) found that age disputes cause substantial stress to young people and have a negative impact on their mental health (Chase *et al.* 2008). This particular question is explored further in chapter 2.

- How can the images of 'youth' be extended to challenge the polarising labels of the 'deserving' vulnerable child 'victim' from the 'undeserving', apparently threatening aggressive young person? In the extreme, this means looking at the split between behaviours that position the young person as a 'victim' at one end of a spectrum and behaviours that position them as a 'perpetrator' of crime at the other end of the spectrum. It is pertinent to address this when a young person is being criminalised for behaviours resulting from coercion and abuse (working in a cannabis factory, for example) or where their perpetration of sexualised bullying may result from previous sexual abuse. Indeed, more recent research into violence among young people in gang-affected neighbourhoods argues that the young person may be both a victim and a perpetrator, and that the crimes they commit may directly result from experiences of intimidation, victimisation, violence and abuse. (Pitts 2008; Firmin 2010; Pearce and Pitts 2011)

Addressing some of these points, Wood *et al.* (2011) prefer to talk about young people as 'instigators' and 'recipients' of violence rather than perpetrators and victims, focusing attention more on the causes of motivation to harm and examining where these motivations might have come from. This is helpful as it encourages consideration of why a young person may harm another, or commit an offence, offering scope to address the impact of abuse and exploitation on a young person's behaviours.

Each chapter of this book engages with aspects of these questions, considering the context for trafficked young people, as explained above.

Outline of the book

This chapter has outlined key debates around the trafficking of young people, and their need to be protected like any other child through safeguarding procedures.

Chapter 2 provides the policy context for work with trafficked young people, identifying some of the central themes and questions that have emerged as knowledge and awareness of the issues has developed. It locates definitions of trafficking within the Palermo Protocol (2000) and explores some of the tensions between understandings of trafficking of young people as an immigration issue as opposed to a child protection issue, as defined by the Protocol. It shows how the exploitation and abuse experienced through the trafficking of young people can be misinterpreted, and therefore hidden under some of the more dominant discourses of 'children on the move' (Herzfeld *et al.* 2006). Exploitation can be overlooked if the young person is described as 'smuggled', a definition that can often sideline the integrated experiences of trafficking that can take place alongside experiences of being smuggled. The chapter also considers how the dominant concerns, often media driven, about the 'sex slave trade' can focus attention on young women and overshadow less 'sexy' forms of trafficking such as trafficking for criminality or for domestic servitude. Without negating the terrible abuse experienced through the sexual exploitation of young women and young men, it argues that this should not occur at the experience of identification of trafficking for other forms of abuse. Finally, the chapter explores the different dynamics taking place within definitions of 'international' trafficking of young people, where movement includes the crossing of country borders, and 'internal' or 'domestic' trafficking, involving the movement of young people, including those born in the UK, within UK borders.

In chapter 3, we explain why and how the research described in the book took place. It explains how agencies supporting sexually exploited children and young people in the UK expressed increasing concern about young people trafficked into or within the UK for the purpose of sexual exploitation. These concerns emerged during 2000 to 2006, at around the same time as the UK Human Trafficking Centre (UKHTC) and the Child Exploitation Online Protection Agency (CEOP) were emerging as police initiatives to protect children from sexual exploitation and trafficking. These initiatives raised awareness of the needs of children and young people trafficked into the UK from abroad. While the UK Home Office and the (then) Department for Children, Schools and Families were producing guidance for practitioners in the field (DCSF 2007), and NGOs such as ECPAT UK (End Child Prostitution, Child Pornography and Trafficking of Children for Sexual Purposes UK) were raising awareness of the children's and young people's needs, it was evident at this stage that no in-depth study had been carried out to explore how, when and why practitioners were identifying young people as trafficked, what resources they were using to work with the trafficked young people and what problems trafficked young people themselves were experiencing in accessing and using resources.

After providing this background rationale for the research, chapter 3 explains how three sites across England took part in the research. The chapter then gives a detailed description of the rationale for qualitative research focusing on identifying practitioners' responses to trafficked young people, explaining the three phases adopted through the research process: the focus groups; the interviews with practitioners; and the case studies of files of individual young people. The ethical implications of conducting such research are explored, reiterating why one-to-one interviews with young people were not considered to be viable for this particular research.

Chapter 4 highlights how trafficking is usually a process that can occur over the longer term, rather than being a one-off event in the life of a young person. Drawing on findings from the research, the processes of trafficking are examined. It is argued that understanding trafficking as a process results in also understanding that the identification of a trafficked young person is a process, not a 'one off' event. Trafficking can be 'hidden' within the young person's day-to-day activities, making it difficult to identify and meaning that information about the abuse may arise through different channels at different times. It is only when information from a range of sources is collected over time that the intricacies and complexities of the abuse can be uncovered.

The chapter continues to explain that once we do understand trafficking as a lengthy, and invariably clandestine, process, we should be led to simultaneously appreciate the need for time for recovery from the experience. Trafficking invariably incorporates physical and emotional abuse, neglect and, often, sexual abuse. These forms of abuse and the control mechanisms used to sustain them have been incorporated into the life of a young person both prior to arrival in the UK and during their time within the UK or pre-departure from the UK. It will be shown how a grasp of these dynamics, many of which occur beyond the national boundaries of the UK, is an essential component in understanding trafficking of young people in its multitude of forms.

Chapter 5 notes that the trafficking of young people is often hidden behind a 'wall of silence', a metaphor we used in our original research summary report to illustrate a phenomenon that prevents children from 'telling' and practitioners from 'hearing' stories of trafficking (Pearce *et al.* 2009). On one side of the wall, trafficked children find it difficult to speak out about their experiences, and on the other side, practitioners can find it difficult to identify and/or believe trafficked young people. The chapter explores this in detail and illustrates, through reference to one specific case example and quotations from interview material and other case study analysis, some of the underlying reasons for the wall of silence.

The research discovered that young people's inability to speak out is linked to many factors, including their own perceptions of abuse and exploitation, their sense of agency, and issues related to post-traumatic stress disorder. While examining these factors, the chapter also refers to debates explored in earlier chapters to develop the importance of a critical awareness of different concepts of 'childhood'. It notes that the concept of 'childhood' in the UK is frequently constructed through a 'Western lens'. The chapter highlights the way standards of child protection vary globally, taking into consideration the employment of many young people in work from a young age in order to contribute to the family income to ensure survival. Thus, what it means to be a young person depends on its particular context, and this context may 'normalise' different behaviours and expectations of young people.

On the other side of the wall, there is a plethora of factors that make it difficult for practitioners to believe and identify trafficked young people. The chapter explores these factors, analysing some of the constraints faced by practitioners in a highly pressurised social work environment which hinder identification. Specifically, the research revealed that some practitioners lack the relevant knowledge, training, experience or resources to identify, work with or refer a trafficked young person. The chapter highlights a 'culture of disbelief', found by the research to permeate practice, whereby young people's stories are heard but not understood.

Chapter 5 concludes by presenting two key arguments. The first is that the culture of disbelief is born out of confusion relating to whether 'child trafficking' is an immigration or a child protection issue. In line with other chapters in the book, it is argued here that trafficking is an extreme form of child abuse and, as such, should be seen first and foremost as a child protection issue. The second argument stresses that young people who have been trafficked from abroad have the same rights under UK child protection legislations as UK citizens. It is paramount that practitioners are made aware of this in order to be able to safeguard trafficked young people better.

Chapter 6 draws on findings from the research to argue that all children's services and related professions have a role to play in identifying and supporting trafficked young people. It argues for joined-up multi-agency services, suggesting that information sharing and collaboration over casework is essential to providing a joined-up response which will keep the young person engaged, safe and well. The chapter identifies specific services, such as education, health and youth offending teams, that have a role to play in helping the trafficked child or young person.

Chapter 7 and chapter 8 both develop the points made in chapter 6, but identify some dedicated specialist services that are needed to address the particular problems experienced by trafficked young people. Chapter 7 focuses specifically on the need for an immediate response to be given to the trafficked young person at the point of entry to the UK. This includes a place of safety and allocation to a statutory 'key worker'. Drawing on ideas developed within social work 'relationship based theory', it looks specifically at the need to support the development of secure relationships between child care workers and the young people concerned. The chapter advocates the provision of a supported and trained key worker who can develop a relationship with the child or young person over time, overseeing their transition into adulthood and 'modelling' a 'good' relationship which will provide a contrast to the young person's abusive and exploitative relationships. Drawing on the important work undertaken by ECPAT and others, summarised in Kelly and Bokhari (2011), the chapter also recognises the need for a Guardian to be allocated for a trafficked child. In addition to focusing specifically on the role of the Guardian, chapter 7 addresses the need for service providers themselves to be able to build a relationship with the young person they are supporting

Chapter 8 continues to look at the need for some dedicated specialist services for trafficked young people. It focuses on the harm and trauma caused by experiences of being trafficked and presses for the young person's therapeutic needs be considered and worked with appropriately. While it endorses the argument made in chapter 6 that all services have an important role to play, and that no one service should be seen to be the only provider for trafficked young people (whether they are trafficked into the UK from abroad or trafficked as UK nationals within the UK), it extends analysis to look in depth at the therapeutic needs of the young people, arguing for a relationship based approach to securing long term well-being. This identifies the need for supported and trained key workers and, in some cases, trained and supported interpreters. The problems faced by interpreters who have inadequate training to understand the emotional and psychological damage experienced by the young person concerned are addressed, along with questions of professional boundaries between interpreter and young person as they emerged in the research.

The chapter addresses the need for safeguarding boards to ensure that foster carers and residential workers are also trained and supported so that they can understand the significance of the role they can play in the young person's life, including securing safety for the child or young person, preventing repeat episodes of 'going missing', and identifying and supporting the treatment of problem emotional behaviours and mental health problems. Integrated within this, the chapter focuses on the need for Child and Adolescent Mental Health Service workers to develop specialist outreach and detached service provision for this client group. It explores the extent of damage that some experiences of exploitation can cause and, in line with the understanding of the process of trafficking as one that takes place over time (as explained in chapters 4 and 5), notes some of the issues raised by practitioners who are trying to support the disclosure and mange the impact of abuse.

Finally, chapter 8 develops the emerging argument that interventions with trafficked young people are best managed through multi-agency work. It highlights some of the complexities that were raised by practitioners from specialist agencies managing multi-agency work with partner agencies. It looks at some of the complexities experienced in gathering and sharing intelligence that can be used as evidence when cases are taken to court to prosecute abusers, exploring the management of boundaries between different agencies. Noting that there may be tensions between different agencies depending upon funding, training and professional focus, the chapter illustrates the need for sustained efforts to enable multi-agency working with trafficked children. It concludes by arguing that while members of all services need to be trained and equipped to work with trafficked children and young people, there are some dedicated services that play a particular role in securing the child's or young person's safety and well-being, but that these need to be fully coordinated through a multi-agency working framework.

Chapter 9 concludes the book, summarising the main themes that have emerged. It notes that research with trafficked young people must take due cognisance of ethical procedures, is best developed in partnership with a service provider and needs mechanisms to offer support to the researchers throughout the process. It highlights how the research has shown that the trafficking of children and young people is a process, hidden behind a wall of silence and within a culture of disbelief. This can be unravelled and exposed to the benefit of children and young people. It clarifies how the research findings suggest that all services have a role to play but that there is a need for some dedicated, relationship based interventions targeted specifically at trafficked children and young people

Finally, chapter 9 explores some of the implications from the research for future practice. It identifies the need to raise awareness that trafficking is a child protection not an immigration issue, arguing for further consideration of the different issues facing children and young people trafficked into the UK from abroad and UK nationals trafficked within and out of the UK. It addresses the need for extended use of protocols and findings from research to reach all practitioners from all professional contexts in all geographical areas so that the lack of awareness, the wall of silence and the culture of disbelief are challenged.

Two key recommendations emerge:

- It is essential to ensure that the process of the trafficking of children and young people, the indicators of trafficking and the implications for the young people concerned are incorporated as essential components within the training of workers for the children's service workforce.
- There is need for the development of ethically sound research with young people who have been trafficked, enabling them to be interviewed and consulted within a safe context and in a way that helps to build their own confidence, knowledge and experience.

Conclusion

In this chapter we have looked at some of the key issues that will figure throughout our book, which is focused on addressing practitioners' responses to trafficked young people. We have introduced the central themes that emerged from our research: that the trafficking of young people is a child protection issue; that concerns have hitherto focused on young women trafficked for sexual exploitation at the expense of encompassing all forms of abuse of both young women and young men; and that it is through supportive relationships with qualified and trained practitioners that identification of a trafficking trajectory can take place. The chapter then looked at some key concepts that reoccur throughout the book. These include assessing what is really meant when we talk of risk and resilience, and what is meant by an age assessment, addressing why understanding this is so important when working with trafficked young people. Finally, this chapter has given an outline of the key points explored within subsequent chapters in the book.

2 The policy context

What is known about child trafficking in the UK

This chapter looks at the contemporary policy context of child trafficking in the UK. It refers to legislation and policy that addresses the trafficking of children, confirming that intervention with children does, according to the UN Convention on the Rights of the Child, include all young people under the age of 18. It draws on this legislation and policy while being mindful that differences do emerge between the needs of young children and those of older young people. The impact of international Conventions on child trafficking is discussed, as well as confusions in the meaning of trafficked, smuggled, unaccompanied asylum-seeking and separated children. The chapter then looks at what is known about the extent and nature of trafficking of children and young people in the UK, raising questions about the method and accuracy of recording processes and exploring some of the tensions that have developed through the recent implementation of the National Referral Mechanism (NRM). It also looks at some of the issues arising from the differences between the trafficking of UK nationals for the purpose of sexual exploitation (as defined in the Sexual Offences Act 2003) and the international trafficking of young people for a variety of forms of exploitation.

In conclusion, this chapter focuses on the continuing limitations to our knowledge about trafficked young people, including gaps between what policy guidance says should happen in response to trafficked children and the reality of practice interventions with young people in the field. It is argued that policy statements and documents remain irrelevant if they exist in a vacuum. In other words, it is only when interventions are resourced, sensitive to the needs of the different groups of young people and properly supported that they have a meaningful impact on a young person's life.

International and national responses to child trafficking

The Protocol to Prevent, Suppress and Punish Trafficking in Persons, especially Women and Children, commonly referred to as the Palermo Protocol

(2000), provided the first internationally agreed definition of human trafficking (Article 3):

> (a) 'Trafficking in persons' shall mean the recruitment, transportation, transfer, harbouring or receipt of persons, by means of the threat or use of force or other forms of coercion, of abduction, of fraud, of deception, of the abuse of power or of a position of vulnerability or of the giving or receiving of payments or benefits to achieve the consent of a person having control over another person, for the purpose of exploitation.

> (b) the consent of a victim of trafficking in persons to the intended exploitation set forth in subparagraph (a) of this article shall be irrelevant where any of the means set forth in subparagraph (a) have been used.

> (c) The recruitment, transportation, transfer, harbouring or receipt of a child for the purposes of exploitation shall be considered 'trafficking in persons' even if this does not involve any of the means set forth in subparagraph (a) of this article.

> (d) Child shall mean any person under the age of 18.

The Palermo Protocol supplements the UN Convention against Transnational Organized Crime and is broadly considered to be the most influential, certainly the most used, international protocol concerning human trafficking. The definition contains three interrelated yet distinct elements: the 'act' of travel (recruitment, transportation and transfer); the 'means' used (use of violence, threats or other use of force or coercion); and the 'purposes' (exploitation which includes, at a minimum, the exploitation or the prostitution of others or other forms of sexual exploitation, forced labour or services, slavery or practices similar to slavery, servitude or the removal of organs).

The Palermo Protocol has been instrumental in shaping debates around 'consent' and 'agency' by stating that children under the age of 18 cannot legally consent to being trafficked. As noted in chapter 1, the UNCRC has also played an important role in ensuring that children under the age of 18 are entitled to specific rights, including the right to be safe from harm and abuse and to receive an education preparing them for healthy adulthood.

Despite the clarity of this definition, there can be confusion about the processes involved in the trafficking of an individual child. For example, the apparent consent and cooperation of the child in being trafficked may be believed, at the expense of looking further and revealing the subtle and/or violent coercion from traffickers hidden behind the veil of consent. The older the young person, the more relevant this is. Assumptions about the young person's capacity to be autonomous and self-directing increase the closer they come to 18. The trafficking of the young person may be a complex part of their migration from war or poverty, involving them in making some decisions about their travel and their future. As such, the processes are complex and simple explanations of how young people may have been 'pushed' into migrating and how the quest for a 'better life' may 'pull' young people into other countries do not adequately explain the various processes at play. Trafficking will be dependent on international patterns of migration and the constraining and enabling factors governing pre-existing migration routes. Further constraints on pre-existing migration routes will increase the potential for young people to remain hidden, invisible and exploited.

The implications of this in practice are developed further in chapters 4 and 5. In such situations, trafficked young people are frequently labelled as being 'smuggled'. 'Trafficking' and 'smuggling' are the two most common terms used for the illegal movement of people. They are often confused, being used interchangeably in practice, something we explore further in chapter 4. A position paper by the Separated Children in Europe Programme and Save the Children, 'Preventing and Responding to Trafficking of Children in Europe', observes:

> 'Since trafficking in human beings involves moving persons for profit, it is often confused – in policy as well as in practice – with smuggling of migrants, which is the subject of another Protocol supplementing the UN Convention against Transnational Organized Crime.
>
> (2007: 9)

According to the Protocol against the Smuggling of Migrants by Land, Sea and Air:

> 'Smuggling of migrants' shall mean the procurement, in order to obtain, directly or indirectly, a financial or other material benefit, of the illegal entry of a person into a State Party of which the person is not a national or a permanent resident.
>
> (United Nations 2000: Article 3)

While the terms 'trafficking' and 'smuggling' have been used interchangeably, there are a number of important distinctions between the two concepts. According to UK government guidance, *Safeguarding Children Who May Have Been Trafficked* (DCSF 2007), 'human smuggling' describes an event whereby 'immigrants' or 'asylum seekers' pay people to help them enter the country illegally, after which there is no longer a relationship between the parties. Trafficked persons, in contrast, are coerced or deceived by the person arranging their relocation, being forced into exploitation. Control of the victim is continuously exerted by the trafficker or person to whom they are delivered or sold during transportation and/or on arrival in the country of destination (Home Office 2011). Thus the relationship between the smuggler and the smuggled person technically ends on entry into the country of destination. In contrast, when a person is trafficked, exploitative relationships continue.

Another distinction relates to the crossing of borders. While smuggling always involves the illegal crossing of an international border, trafficking can be internal (within a country) as well as transnational (Save the Children 2007:10). Legally speaking, trafficking constitutes a violation of human rights, whereas smuggling constitutes a crime against a state. Under UK law, smuggling is referred to as 'facilitation' and is an offence under the Asylum and Immigration Act 2003.

While a clear distinction can be made at the conceptual level, boundaries between the two terms often become blurred in practice (see chapter 4 for more details). Although the crime of smuggling does not constitute a human rights violation in itself, smuggled persons are also often victims of human rights violations. Moreover, some cases may involve elements of both crimes: for instance, a migrant may be smuggled into a country and later deceived, transported further and forced into trafficking and exploitation (Save the Children 2007: 10).

Children and forced migration: the 'process' of children on the move

Although by no means a new phenomenon, human 'trafficking' and 'smuggling' have risen up the policy agendas of many countries since the end of the Cold War. Arguably, this has been as a result of efforts to control migration and contain refugees in regions of origin. The right to seek asylum has, in recent years, been operating in the context of a shrinkage of 'asylum space', making many forms of migration necessarily more clandestine (Castles 2002; Morrison 2002). As a result, for adults, children and young people fleeing persecution, the use of 'smuggling' networks may be the only way for refugees and migrants to reach Europe, given that restrictive asylum legislation and policy deny access to all but a tiny percentage of refugees. Castles (2002) has also suggested that these restrictive policies have consequently created opportunities for agents and brokers to facilitate 'smuggling' and/or 'trafficking'.

Richmond (1994) examined the dynamics of migration, placing voluntary and forced migration along a continuum of 'proactive' and 'reactive' migration. Central to this continuum is the recognition of the sense of agency of those migrating. Richmond argued that any form of migration involves differing degrees of voluntary or 'proactive' and forced or 'reactive' elements which intersect with prevailing global political and economic circumstances (see also Kunz 1973). Trafficking, including for forced labour, is a form of forced migration that tends towards the 'reactive' rather than 'proactive' end of any such continuum, with individuals put under economic, social and political pressures over which they have very little control (Richmond 1994).

For young people who are trafficked, these pressures and lack of power over them are particularly present. Additionally, young people may be controlled by adults who have intimate knowledge of their background and history, using this knowledge to exploit the young person over time. If this knowledge results in a young person believing that it is in their own best interests to accompany a trafficker, what may initially have been perceived as being a proactive choice may, once they realise they have been deceived or betrayed by their traffickers, become a situation of forced or 'reactive' migration. Certainly trafficking incorporates aspects of forced migration beyond simple, monocausal 'push' or 'pull' explanations and should be considered as a dynamic and changeable phenomenon.

It has been suggested that the analysis of young people's movement within and between countries is limited and that the focus on trafficking as a criminal act has downplayed the issues of why and how children migrate (Reale 2008). Save the Children, for example, argues that this denies attention being given to how 'children on the move' can be protected other than by the prevention of movement in the first place. Reale (2008) suggests that children's and young people's movement is multidimensional, with both negative and positive outcomes, and that 'children on the move' are particularly vulnerable to exploitation and abuse, especially those travelling unaccompanied. It is also the case that children and young people migrating with their families may not necessarily be safe from harm if parents are unable to secure basic rights (O'Connell Davidson and Farrow 2007).

In contrast, it has been suggested that the experiences of young people who migrate may ultimately bring them benefits. Sigona and Hughes (2010) suggest that opening up research on 'trafficked children', 'unaccompanied minors' and 'separated children' to other 'undocumented' children and young people would enable us to problematise immigration regimes. O'Connell Davidson (2005) expresses concern that the child trafficking lens turns children and young people into passive objects and eternal victims. Importantly, this deflects attention from more structural issues such as immigration regimes. Again, although this literature refers to children under the age of 18 as a homogeneous group, each of the points it makes becomes more apparent in considering the impact on young people, many of whom may be assumed to possess adult qualities and capacities. Overall, in our call for practitioners to better understand the reasons why young people move, we suggest that interventions responding to abuse and exploitation need to consider each stage of a young person's movement within an overall appreciation of potential structural issues relating to causes of migration.

Having said this, young people may be forced, coerced or deceived into migration. This 'trafficking' across international borders for the purposes of exploitation is invariably based on the young person's position of vulnerability and accompanied by a betrayal by adults in positions of trust. The Palermo Protocol explicitly recognises these positions of vulnerability and, as shown above, provides an influential and authoritative definition directing responses in the UK towards such cases.

Within the literature on adult and child trafficking, differing discourses that guide our understanding of the trafficking of young people include human rights, migration management and organised crime perspectives (Morrison 2002). Discourses oscillate between these perspectives, expanding and contracting over time (Bovarnick 2010). The human rights perspective takes in two centuries of the anti-slavery movement, with the trafficking of children and young people being approached from an international 'child slavery' perspective in recent years (Craig *et al.*2007; Craig 2010). Child trafficking has been referred to as a modern form of child slavery (Buck and Nicholson 2010; van de glind 2010). As with the trafficking of women, there are heated debates between 'abolitionists' (those who aim to abolish all prostitution on the grounds that it exploits the women and men involved) and supporters of 'sex workers' rights' (those who defend the decision to sell sex for money, particularly when local and global poverty means there are few other alternatives), each side using the term 'trafficking' in different ways and for different ends (Anderson and O'Connell Davidson 2004). For example, sexual trafficking has been problematised by O'Connell Davidson (2005), who positions the exploitation of children in prostitution as a problem of unequal power and unequal distribution of wealth. She advocates that the young person's agency and self-determinism be understood as contributors to decisions to sell sex. Others, such as Buck and Nicholson (2010), prefer to focus on the impact of exploitation and abuse within a 'slavery' discourse which, by default, focuses on the young person as a victim and overlooks recognition of the impact of their own agency and self-determinism.

Irrespective of these tensions, the so-called management of migration during the 1990s saw the overriding policy agendas of the governments of Europe and North America focus on deterrence of migrants (Bloch and Schuster 2005; Sales 2007; Solomos 2003; Zetter *et al.* 2003). Also, by the late 1990s, trafficking and smuggling were firmly framed in issues of transnational organised crime agendas (Morrison 2002) and it was from this context that the Palermo Protocol emerged.

The Protocol did not therefore emerge from debates on the rights of children and young persons, and this limitation is not widely considered. It was the organised crime perspective of trafficking that was invoked, for example, in September 2001 when the torso of a young boy named by police officers as 'Adam' was found in the River Thames in London. During subsequent investigations by police, the link between the boy and human trafficking for the purposes of ritual killing was invoked. This organised crime perspective was also invoked with the disappearance of Madeleine McCann in 2007. Such events shape debates on trafficking in the UK as well as illustrate just how complex and dynamic forms of trafficking can be.

Unaccompanied asylum-seeking children and separated children

If a separated young person is identified, they are invariably referred to an asylum team and thereby become part of what is commonly referred to as the unaccompanied asylum-seeking children (UASC) population. Trafficked young people, travelling in the context of exploitation, can have their experiences hidden through the UASC label. It is therefore important to clarify the meaning of UASC further to explore how this may occur.

UASC is the term most commonly used by local authorities to describe children and young people arriving in the UK seeking asylum without the presence of a parent or designated carer. If the young person is not immediately recognised as trafficked, they may be absorbed into the UASC category by default. Figures suggest that boys and young men are disproportionally represented in figures of UCAS children looked after by the local authority. Although the trafficking of children is often seen through a gendered and sexualised lens, with predominant interest in girls and young women trafficked for sexual exploitation (Doezema 2010), this gendered focus is not reflected in data of separated and UAS children. As of 31 March 2011, 65,520 children were looked after by local authorities, 2,370 of whom were UASC. Of the 65,520 looked-after children, 56 per cent (36,470) were boys and 44 per cent (29,050) were girls, while 89 per cent of the unaccompanied asylum-seeking children were boys and 11 per cent were girls (Department for Education 2011, noted in BAAF 2012).

While the figures are informative, it has been argued that a literal interpretation can be misleading. As noted, in the UK, separated young people who have applied for asylum are commonly referred to as UASC. However, using this terminology to describe young people who arrive in the UK without an accompanying adult is problematic and contested. The term 'UASC' fails to include those young people who are accompanied by an adult who is not their parent, guardian or primary carer. The Separated Children in

Europe Programme refers to such young people as 'separated children' (2009: 3). While many local authorities frequently use the term 'UASC', it sits uncomfortably with some as it is feared that the asylum-seeking status can take precedence over the young person's status as a child in need.

'Separated children' is the term used in most countries to describe children who are outside their country of origin and separated from their parents or legal or customary primary carer (Joint Committee on Human Rights 2007). The use of this term is seen as good practice, since it describes the situation of many unaccompanied asylum-seeking children as being separated from their families abroad, and is recognised as embracing the needs of all young people up to the age of 18. ECPAT also refers to 'separated children', as the term denotes all those who are separated from their parents or primary guardian (ECPAT UK 2011b; Kelly and Bokhari 2011). However, as noted in chapter 1, while it is assumed that the generic term 'children' embraces all young people under the age of 18, as in the UNCRC, the tendency is for 'children' to imply younger rather than older children, focusing the lens on those under, rather than over 10 years of age. As a result, the specific needs of teenagers, particularly those approaching 18, may at best be overlooked or, at worst, assumed to conflate with adulthood.

In this book we use the term 'separated children' rather than UASC, accepting that in this context 'children' embraces young people up to 18 years of age. However, as local authority data are recorded under the category of UASC, with references to UASC and to separated children sometimes made interchangeably, the term UASC will emerge occasionally throughout the text. We will also refer to the emerging literature on 'undocumented migrant minors' that seeks to open up research to other forms of child migration beyond 'trafficked children' or 'unaccompanied asylum seekers' (Sigona and Hughes 2010).

UK legislative and policy framework

'Trafficking' has been written into various domestic laws within the UK. Sections 57 to 59 of the Sexual Offences Act 2003 cover trafficking into, within and out of the UK for the purposes of sexual exploitation. Sections 4 and 5 of the Asylum and Immigration (Treatment of Claimants etc.) Act 2004 made it an offence to facilitate the trafficking of people for exploitation. There is also other specialist legislation such as the Gangmasters Licensing Act 2005, which aims to better protect migrant workers. Trafficking involves the committing of many other offences. For law enforcement purposes there are advantages to using the specific offence of trafficking, but this does not imply that other offences should be ignored. Traffickers can be charged and prosecuted with many other related offences such as 'facilitation', 'rape', 'abduction' and 'grievous bodily harm', to name a few. While the use of criminal law is not always successful, it is important to note the essential role that these options can play in disrupting and prosecuting traffickers, interrupting or preventing further abuse of young people.

Other laws that are relevant specifically to the trafficking of children and young people include the Children Acts 1989 and 2004. The principles around safeguarding children from abuse outlined within the Children Acts are identified in the UK Action Plan on Tackling Human Trafficking (see Home Office 2008b). The UK government also produced guidance on safeguarding children who may have been trafficked (DCSF 2007). This provides a range of flow charts to guide practitioners through the use of sections 17, 20 and 47 of the Children Act 1989, setting a framework for preventing the inappropriate use of private foster care arrangements. In addition, the UK Staying Safe Action Plan notes the need to improve the provision of a 'safety net' and of safe places for children who go missing from home (DCSF 2008a: 45). For fear of exhausting a point, it is worth noting again that these guidance frameworks assume homogeneity between younger and older children, overlooking the specific dynamics that can occur for teenagers during a period in their lifespan development that brings them closer to adulthood. Issues such as seeking independence from the parental or care home, furthering independent study and /or finding employment, and experimenting with interpersonal and sexual relationships create particular dynamics in practice that differ from those in interventions designed to support younger children. Each of these issues calls for a different approach to engage with the young person and to support their developing sense of agency while ensuring their safety. Indeed, the focus needs to be more on supporting them to help themselves in developing tools to stay safe, rather than developing means to 'rescue' them from harm.

These guidance frameworks have been developed by some local authorities to refine specific areas of practice. For example, the London Safeguarding Children Board has produced its own protocol for safeguarding trafficked and exploited children, giving guidance to professionals and volunteers from all agencies in safeguarding children abused and neglected by adults who traffic them into and out of the UK. It has also produced a 'London toolkit' (2011) for safeguarding trafficked children, providing guidance on employing some of the sophisticated methods needed to put the aim of safeguarding trafficked children into effect. Some aspects of these revised guidance frameworks do concern themselves with the changing demands presented by young people as they progress towards adulthood, particularly where cases of disputed age need to be addressed. However, a comprehensive understanding of the impact of adolescence on the vulnerability of trafficked young people is yet to be developed.

In 2011 the UK government published *Human Trafficking: The Government's Strategy* (Home Office 2011), which dedicated chapter 7 to a focus on 'child' trafficking. This document places a stronger focus on identifying and working with source countries as a method of tackling child trafficking, and notes examples of good practice from local authorities working closely with the police in order that support for victims accompanies interventions to attempt to identify and prosecute traffickers. This builds from the government's ratification of the Council of Europe Convention on Action against Trafficking of 17 December 2008, which became operational on 1 April 2009. The Convention is designed both to promote action against traffickers and, equally importantly, to provide safeguards and entitlements to identified victims of trafficking. It is the first international treaty that obliges states to adopt minimum standards to assist trafficked persons and protect their rights (Anti-Trafficking Monitoring Group 2010).

The Convention recognises the difficulties faced by law enforcement and social care professionals in making positive identifications of victims, given the covert nature of the crime and the reluctance of many victims to disclose their plight to the authorities. It recognises that victims may fear retribution from the traffickers or lack trust in the willingness or ability of the authorities to protect them. The Convention notes that European Union member states must provide the opportunity for a 'reflection period' to be given to victims whose entry into the country may well have been irregular and where otherwise they would be subject to removal by immigration authorities. The reflection period in the UK is 45 days (exceeding the prescribed minimum of 30 days) where 'reasonable grounds' have been established by a 'competent authority' that an individual should be considered to be a victim. The task for collecting data on trafficked children is assigned to two 'competent authorities': the UK Border Agency (UKBA) and the UKHTC. Together they are responsible for the National Referral Mechanism (NRM), introduced in 2009 as a two-step decision-making process for identifying all victims of human trafficking, including adults and children.

The two stages start with a 'first responder', which includes designated representatives from police, social and children's services, the NSPCC and Barnardo's: all authorised to refer potential child victims of trafficking to the competent authorities. The second stage involves these competent authorities making, within five days, a 'reasonable ground' decision of whether the child has been trafficked. If a positive reasonable ground decision is made, the victim is granted a 45-day reflection period and the competent authority will further investigate in order to reach a 'conclusive grounds' decision (see CEOP, NSPCC CTAIL and UKHTC 2011).

Criticisms have been levelled at the effective use of the NRM as a mechanism for recording data of trafficked children and young people, or indeed, as a mechanism for effecting genuine safeguarding strategies. These concerns include worry about limited awareness of the existence of the NRM among potential referral agencies; worry that referral to the NRM may result in further interrogation of the young person about their circumstances, causing them additional stress; and worry that a mistaken rejection of a 'reasonable or conclusive ground' would further undermine the young person's confidence in being believed.

As is explored further in this book, and as is clearly illustrated by work with foster carers who are providing support for trafficked children (Fursland 2009), it may take a young person a long time to disclose enough information about their experiences of being trafficked to confirm conclusive grounds. Indeed, the review by the Anti-Slavery Alliance of the use of the National Referral Mechanism showed poor identification and recording of cases of trafficking of both genders, little understanding of the child protection needs of trafficked children, and only an oversimplified awareness of the different experiences children may have of 'childhood' and 'home' (Anti-Trafficking Monitoring Group 2010). (There is further analysis in chapter 5 of this book, and in Brueil 2008, Reale 2008 and Every and Augoustinos 2007, of how the dominant, Western, Eurocentric concept of 'home' may limit understanding of the diverse experiences of children who are trafficked from countries where war, poverty and natural disasters prevail.)

One of the main findings of the study by the Anti-Trafficking Monitoring Group (2010) was that the UK government's anti-trafficking practice was not compliant with the Council of Europe Convention on Action against Trafficking in Human Beings (drawn up in 2005). In relation to children they found that the UK government was not compliant either with other aspects of UK law or with best practice. All of these concerns have meant that there is open acknowledgement that the data recorded through both NGOs and NRM underreport and misrepresent actual figures of trafficked children (CEOP 2011).

In relation to child victims of trafficking (i.e. those up to age 18), Article 10 of the Council of Europe Convention on Action against Trafficking in Human Beings (2005) requires member states to ensure that victims are provided with accommodation, legal advice, medical assistance and education; that an 'organisation, authority or individual' be appointed to act as a guardian; and that all decisions regarding the child's welfare and future should be taken in their 'best interests' in accordance with the UNCRC. This is in line with the expectations of current practice, where all separated children, whatever their country of origin or residential status, should become looked-after children within the provision of the 1989 and 2004 Children Acts. Local Safeguarding Children Boards (LSCBs), the multi-agency framework to facilitate the collaboration of child protection, health, education and statutory and voluntary youth service providers in the safeguarding of children and young people in each local authority area, should provide the location where trafficked children are identified and protected in the same way as any child who is at risk of harm and abuse. It is evident that despite appropriate policy guidance and frameworks, the reality in practice may still leave much to be desired (CEOP 2011; ECPAT UK 2011b)

Trafficked children leaving care: UK local initiatives

The Children (Leaving Care) Act 2000 introduced amendments to the Children Act 1989 regarding leaving care provisions and specified duties of local authorities with respect to children who have been 'looked after' by them in the past. Local authorities have a duty to give 'former relevant children' assistance by devising pathway plans, outlining support and accommodation, and to provide education/training or support for those seeking employment. Local authorities further have a duty to contribute to expenses incurred by the young person who is living near the place where they are employed or seeking employment, or receiving education or training.

With regard to separated (UASC) children and young people there is a degree of uncertainty among local authorities as to whether the above-mentioned leaving care provisions apply. However, court intervention has clarified that a child who has been accepted as 'looked after' should be eligible for leaving care services (including a named personal adviser, accommodation, and a pathway plan) irrespective of the decision on the young person's asylum claim.

To assist local authorities in meeting leaving care costs of separated children and young people, the government has set up a UASC Leaving Care Costs Grant (DCSF 2007). Trafficked children and young people often enter the care system either through asylum teams or sexual exploitation services. As such, their care entitlements frequently overlap with those of UASC. Where a young person's asylum claim has failed, even when a period of limited leave is granted it is likely that he or she will ultimately be removed from the UK. In such an event, the local authority must still provide the leaving care services to which the young person is entitled. How this is implemented and whether the funds allocated are sufficient to cover the costs involved are other questions that have been raised in a number of quarters (Anti-Trafficking Monitoring Group 2010).

Age assessments: determining the age of a child

One of the central questions behind the interventions noted above is whether the child is acknowledged to be a child. This is of central concern for work with young people who may be approaching the age of 18. Many separated (UASC) children who are entitled to statutory support become caught in a process of 'age dispute' that further hampers the process of settlement and recovery. Questions about the appropriate use of 'age assessments' of young people who may have been trafficked have been raised by Crawley (2007), who looks at the damaging impact of techniques used to assess the child's age. Guidelines for good practice specifying that child protection responses precede questions of age dispute are being overlooked (Aynsley-Green 2007).

There is a growing number of looked after unaccompanied asylum-seeking children aged 16 and older with little certainty of what their status will be once they reach 18. At this stage, the legal status of a young person is assessed and their future will largely depend on whether the young person is granted refugee status, humanitarian protection, discretionary leave, or whether the young person's asylum application is rejected. If awarded 'refugee' status, the young person will be entitled to all rights as enshrined in the 1951 Refugee Convention. Humanitarian protection and discretionary leave are awarded for temporary admission, with no rights for family reunification. In 2010, the total number of unaccompanied children under the age of 17 to be granted 'refugee' status was 264; 11 were granted humanitarian protection; 1,096 were granted discretionary leave. The number of young people refused any form of status was 317. The numbers and characteristics for unaccompanied young people under 18 who reached the age of 18 for the same year of 2010 tell a different story: of a total of 671 children, 88 per cent (590) were refused any form of status, with 63 granted refugee status, 1 humanitarian protection and 17 discretionary leave (Home Office 2010). Therefore, where a claim for asylum has failed, even when a period of limited leave is granted, it is likely that the young person will ultimately be removed from the UK. In such an event, the local authority must still provide the leaving care services to which the young person is entitled.

There has always been a tension between immigration control, the immigration status of the child and child protection concerns. However, following the Palermo Protocol, and subsequent developments in good practice, it is clear that child protection should be the first and foremost consideration when working with a case of a trafficked young person. The lifting of the UK government's reservation to the UNCRC in December 2008 is significant as it demonstrates a total commitment to a child-centred approach, protecting children from exploitation (DCSF 2008b). Although separated (UCAS) young people had been eligible for protection under section 17 or 20 of the Children Act 1989, lifting the reservation made a definite statement that trafficked young people will receive the same protection under the current safeguarding children's framework as other children in the UK. To be effective, this must include a child-centred approach to age assessment.

While these decisions have been welcomed, NGOs such as Amnesty International and the Refugee Council are continuing to campaign for greater recognition of the needs of trafficked people, particularly children and young people. Specifically, they call for:

- appropriate support and accommodation with specialist providers to deal with victims;
- making funding available to voluntary and statutory agencies to provide specialist support to trafficked people and particularly children;
- investment in research to establish a clearer picture of the prevalence of trafficking and characteristics and needs of victims of trafficking.

The extent and nature of trafficking of young people in the UK

As has been noted above, the identification and recording of trafficked young people are inadequate and confused. This means that data on trafficked young people are misleading and are not a true reflection of the scale of the problem. One of the problems in recording accurate data is in ensuring that a balanced picture is given, without bias towards one form of trafficking, such as trafficking for sexual exploitation, over another, such as trafficking for domestic servitude, for example.

It has long been argued that the dominant concern of a 'sex slave trade' and 'child sexual exploitation' has overshadowed concern about (and therefore awareness of) children and young people who are trafficked for other forms of exploitation (Jobe 2008, 2010; Pearce *et al.* 2009). UK studies by CEOP (2007, 2009, 2011), Harris and Robinson (2007) and ECPAT UK (2007, 2009b, 2010, 2011a, 2011b) reveal that while many young women, and some young men, are known to be trafficked for sexual exploitation, there is a broad range of reasons for being trafficked into the country and that it is rare for exploitation to fit neatly into one category. The Home Office report *Trafficking for the Purposes of Labour Exploitation* gives an overview of existing literature on other forms of exploitation experienced by trafficked persons, much of which is overshadowed by media interest in the 'sex slave trade' (Dowling *et al.* 2007). Dwyer *et al.* (2011) have also investigated the links between immigration status and migrants' vulnerability to forced labour. This work illustrates the complex interrelationship between forms of abuse and exploitation, arguing against a simple demarcation between methods and purposes of the trafficking of human beings and identifying the danger in focusing on just one form or purpose of trafficking.

It is clearly not helpful when a media drive for 'sexy' headlines creates a 'hierarchy' of concern about abuse, raising public interest in sexual abuse at the expense of concern about domestic servitude or forced criminality, for example. The research in the field demonstrates that young people are trafficked for a plethora of forms of exploitation which are invariably merged and interchangeable. Importantly, while practitioners and the general public may be unaware of the range and nature of abuse, so too may the victims themselves: many of the young people concerned do not recognise the nature of the abuse they are subjected to. The forms of exploitation are frequently referred to as 'three d-jobs' – dirty, difficult and dangerous (see OHCHR 2012 for further detail). They include:

- sexual exploitation
- domestic labour
- benefit fraud
- work in cannabis factories
- work in restaurants
- work in factories
- work in nail bars
- drug mules or decoys for adult drug traffickers
- begging or pickpocketing
- forced marriage
- trade in human organs (although, as far as is known, no cases of this have emerged within the UK to date)
- ritual killings (the 'Adam' torso in the River Thames has been mentioned as a possible case of trafficking)
- agricultural labour
- illegal intercountry adoption
- trafficking of children as a 'repayment of debt'.

The UK has been identified as a significant transit and destination country for children trafficked for a range of different reasons. The majority of children and young people trafficked into the UK begin their journey in East Asia or Africa (Sillen and Beddoe 2007). That said, particular economic and political changes within Europe have contributed to specific forms of feminised poverty, resulting in an increasing movement of impoverished young people within and between European countries (Mullenger 2000; CEOP 2011). The full scope of trafficking remains unknown because of its clandestine and transient nature. Reliable data are still relatively scarce to give a comprehensive overview of the trafficking of young people in the UK.

In 2006, the first proactive policing operation, Pentameter 1, was launched to tackle human trafficking, involving all 55 police forces simultaneously across the UK. The operation visited 515 premises, identified 188 women, primarily from Eastern Europe, China/Southeast Asia, Africa or Brazil, confirming 84 of these women as victims of trafficking. As less than 10 per cent of the UK's massage parlours and brothels were visited during Pentameter, it is therefore estimated that several thousand more victims remain to be found. While the majority of the women discovered by Pentameter 1 were aged between 18 and 25 at the time of their arrest, 12 were minors aged between 14 and 17. The operation resulted in 232 people being arrested and 134 people being charged with a variety of offences (Operation Pentameter 2006).

Building on Pentameter 1, a further operation, Pentameter 2, was launched on 3 October 2007. This identified 167 victims of trafficking for sexual exploitation, and 13 of these were found to be children. In its 2008 *Update to the UK Action Plan on Tackling Human Trafficking*, the Home Office gave figures from Pentameter 2, which it said was:

> mounted on a larger scale than Pentameter 1 and lasted for twice as long. During the operational phase of the campaign 822 premises were visited of which 582 were residential, 157 were massage parlours or saunas and 83 were other premises including hotels and ports of entry into the UK. 528 arrests were made and 167 victims of sexual exploitation were recovered, of which 13 were children/young people . . . In addition, 5 victims of labour trafficking were recovered, of which 3 were children/young people.
>
> (2008b: 17)

In 2007, CEOP published a scoping study on child trafficking in the UK, which found 330 cases of children who fitted the profile of having been trafficked. Of the children found in this scoping study, 276 (84 per cent) were believed to be between 15 and 17 years old; 24 were thought to be between 13 and 14; 14 were 12 years old or younger; the age of the remaining 16 was not known. These findings may be questioned as many of the children's ages were estimated through age assessments, rather than through verified documented evidence. In this way, it may also be the case that some adult cases may relate to children.

Of the 330 cases, the majority (86 per cent) of children with clear evidence of trafficking were girls; 65 per cent of these girls were believed to have been trafficked for the purpose of sexual exploitation, while 23 per cent were suspected to have been trafficked for the purpose of domestic servitude. The remainder were thought to have been trafficked for the purposes of drug trafficking, cannabis cultivation and other forms of criminal activity, adoption, servile marriages, benefit fraud and other forms of labour exploitation such as in restaurants. The types of exploitation in the cases of trafficked boys recorded in the study were less clear. The report suggests that this may be because boys were being smuggled into the UK, rather than trafficked, or because the types of exploitation boys experienced were harder to identify. Cases where information regarding the exploitation of boys was given included those involving cannabis cultivation, labour exploitation, begging and domestic servitude. In total, 44 source countries were identified in the study, mainly in the regions of the Far East, Southeast Asia, Central Asia, South Asia, West Africa, East Africa, Eastern Europe and the Baltic states (CEOP 2007: 5).

ECPAT UK (2007) found similar patterns in its study of 80 suspected cases of trafficked young people coming from Africa and East Asia. Similarly, 38 of the 50 young people who were suspected of being trafficked in a review of trafficked and sexually exploited young people in West Sussex were 16 or 17 years old. Of those whose origin was known, 62 per cent (21) of whom were of Chinese origin, 12 were from Liberia and 7 were from India. Most presented as separated children, either as unaccompanied minors or with adults who were not holding parental responsibility for them (Harris and Robinson 2007).

A Strategic Threat Assessment from CEOP (April 2009) identified 325 children from 52 countries as potential victims of trafficking (March 2007 to February 2008). Disaggregating child trafficking by nationality, the report highlighted key points and the 'profiles' of particular nationalities. Information known to date about trafficked children from China, West and East Africa, Afghanistan, Vietnam, Bangladesh, South Africa and Zimbabwe, as well as Roma children and 'internally' trafficked UK nationals, was provided to begin to identify the known trends of child trafficking within the UK. In line with findings from other reviews, the assessment also found that sexual exploitation is likely to be the most identifiable form of trafficking. Noting that children who are trafficked often come from vulnerable or socio-economically deprived backgrounds, it also described how violence, or the threat of violence, is just one of the many control mechanisms used by traffickers to silence children or young people.

Research commissioned by the Office of the Children's Commissioner for Wales and carried out by ECPAT UK considered the evidence base for child trafficking in Wales (ECPAT 2009a). The experiences of 41 practitioners in Cardiff, Newport, Swansea and Wrexham were examined and, of 45 children reported to be of concern, 32 children within Wales were included in the study. For the first time, more boys than girls were identified as having been trafficked and it was also confirmed that children were being identified in rural towns and villages as well as the more expected urban areas close to airports. The report highlighted how practitioners often encountered difficulties identifying a child as trafficked, stemming from attitudes, knowledge and practice on or about trafficking more broadly.

While centralised asylum and immigration legislation and policy remain in non-devolved areas, services for children within Wales are the responsibility of the Welsh Government, and the Welsh Assembly has now set up a Cross-Party Group on Trafficking of Women and Children.

The most recent data produced by CEOP *et al.* (2011) show that in total 202 children have been identified as trafficked from 36 countries over the period from 1 January to 15 September 2011, a figure including referrals to the NRM and by CTAIL. With advance warning that this is a 'snapshot' and recognising the problems discussed above about the identification, referral and recording of trafficked children, the data show that 67 had been trafficked from African countries, mainly girls trafficked for sexual exploitation; 63 from Asian countries, including 48 boys trafficked from Vietnam for labour exploitation and cannabis cultivation; 50 from Eastern Europe, trafficked mainly for benefit fraud and criminal exploitation; and 4 trafficked from China. The data show that children's experience of trafficking took place over multiple journeys and was for multiple forms of exploitation.

As noted, scoping exercises carried out into the extent of trafficking of children and young people suggest that there is better identification and reporting of young people trafficked for sexual exploitation than for other forms of exploitation. Cases of trafficking of young people into the country for domestic servitude are underreported, invariably remaining 'hidden' under private fostering arrangements and/or through the entrapment of the child within the home (Fursland 2009; Hughes and Owen 2009). In addition, the impact of poverty and global inequalities on young people (Melrose 2010) and of issues facing young men trafficked into the country for work in cannabis factories is poorly understood, with the young men being criminalised, and often incarcerated, for committing offences instead of being understood as having been exploited. Indeed, other research into work with boys and young men shows the detrimental impact of gendered perceptions, a binary opposition between female victims and male perpetrators of crime and disorder which means that boys' vulnerability to sexual abuse and exploitation is overlooked (Lillywhite and Skidmore 2006).

Young people going missing

One of the central worries for practitioners and policy makers aiming to support trafficked young people is in addressing the problem of trafficked young people 'going missing'. Work by E. Kelly and Bokhari (2011), Crawley (2006), Sillen and Beddoe (2007), Beddoe (2007) and ECPAT UK (2009b) note poor identification of the full range of cases of trafficking of young people, suggesting a significant underreporting of cases, many of which are cases where the child has 'gone missing'.

CEOP estimated that 56 per cent of the 330 known or suspected trafficked children identified in their scoping study had gone missing without trace (CEOP 2007). Of the trafficked children who went missing and were later found, there was suspicion or evidence that abuse had occurred in the intervening period. The study further highlights failings in social welfare arrangements for these children. Prior to the launch of the CEOP scoping study, the UK government had announced that 220 victims of child trafficking had been identified over an 18-month period. Of these 220 children, 183 went missing from social service care (Sillen and Beddoe 2007). This supports a claim made in an ECPAT UK study on missing children published in 2007 that 60 per cent – or 48 out of 80 reported or suspected cases of child trafficking – had gone missing. This study was based on interviews with practitioners from three specific regions in the UK, suggesting that many children who have gone missing after being trafficked into the country 'had not been investigated, identified or recorded as victims of trafficking at the time they went missing' (ECPAT UK 2007: 5). The report reveals a worrying lack of data held on the 80 children suspected of having been trafficked into the UK. Similarly, the review of young people in West Sussex who had been trafficked into the UK noted that over half of the 50 cases went missing within a week of arrival (Harris and Robinson 2007). This work noted that, since 2000, 118 UASC had gone missing from care in West Sussex and that over half were suspected victims of trafficking.

'Internal', 'domestic' and 'international' trafficking

Studies of migration have often split into two different bodies of work – one primarily concerned with the international trafficking of children and young people between countries, and the other concerned with the 'internal' or 'domestic' trafficking of children and young people within countries. It has been argued that these two different approaches to understanding migration generally have remained unhelpfully separated from each other (King *et al.* 2008). As a result, different sources of data and different research techniques have been used to describe international and internal migration, often led by policy agendas between or within countries. This narrows our understanding of migration, including the process of trafficking of children and young people from abroad, a process that includes further movement or trafficking within countries of destination.

In line with the approaches outlined by King *et al.* (2008), our research suggests that 'internal' or 'domestic' trafficking can be understood in the UK to be divided between two strands of children and young people who are trafficked:

- *Children trafficked from abroad and then 'internally trafficked'* These young people will be moved on within the UK after arrival from abroad. They may not speak English, may have little knowledge of the UK support systems available through children's services, and may have come from communities (and climates) that are profoundly different from those in the UK. They may have experienced violence and abuse during their journey and are unlikely to have any knowledge of a local peer group or family/care network that they could have any access to within the UK. As a result, they may be disorientated, displaced and may feel isolated from any support that can be offered to them.

- *Children born in the UK (or who have lived in the UK for a substantial period of time, with UK citizenship) trafficked within the UK* These young people, having been born in the UK (or having lived in the UK for a substantial period of time, with UK citizenship) are officially registered as UK nationals, and in most cases have a history and knowledge of life in the UK. Most of these young people will be English-speaking (as a second if not their first language). They will, in the main, have a knowledge of or familiarity with different forms of UK culture, and will have some awareness of a local peer group, family or care network within the UK. In the main, attention has been focused on UK nationals who have been trafficked for the purpose of sexual exploitation (as outlined in the Sexual Offences Act 2003). Little is known about whether, and to what extent, UK nationals are internally trafficked for other forms of exploitation.

When using the concept of 'internal' or 'domestic ' trafficking it is important that these distinctions are kept in mind so that the unique vulnerabilities and needs of children and young people trafficked into the country from abroad can be taken into account.

Throughout this book we have maintained a dominant focus on the experiences of children and young people who are trafficked into the UK from abroad, while taking note of cases of the 'internal/domestic' trafficking of UK nationals within the country as they arose in the research.

Gaps in existing data

There are still gaps in knowledge around the needs of trafficked persons, particularly children and young people. Existing research paints a complex picture of those needs. The work of Zimmerman *et al.* (2006) explored the health needs of 207 women trafficked into the UK, 24 of whom were aged between 15 and 17. The women in the study had experienced extreme forms of sexual, physical and emotional violence and abuse in their home countries before being trafficked. Zimmerman *et al.* highlighted the detrimental cumulative effect that continued violence experienced during the trafficking process had on women's physical and mental health. They identified important recommendations for health and social service providers across Europe, ranging from the need to provide a recovery and reflection period of a minimum of 90 days for adults after being identified as trafficked, to the need for safe housing, long-term psychological support, and occupational and educational training.

Recent research on the emotional well-being and mental health of separated children in the UK mentions the extreme trauma, distress and accumulated loss of family members experienced by many young people before leaving their country of origin or during their journeys (Chase *et al.* 2008: 2). Children, particularly older children participating in the research, suffered from anxieties, stress and other difficulties linked to emotional health problems. The work reported a range of common manifestations of emotional difficulties, ranging from missing family, feelings of isolation and loneliness, disturbed sleep patterns, general anxiety, headaches, panic attacks, depression, eating difficulties and, in some cases, more severe mental health problems requiring specialist support or hospitalisation. While this research revealed gaps in terms of appropriate (mental) health services, it also highlighted the need to develop an appropriate language for mental health that is less stigmatising and better understood by young people across a range of cultures. Many participants articulated their feelings of loss and trauma as a 'sickness of the heart, not of the mind' (Chase *et al.* 2008: 3). Because trafficking often involves every form of abuse – neglect, physical, sexual and emotional abuse – it is argued that many symptoms may be an entirely normal response to what is, essentially, an abnormal situation (P. Hynes 2009). Westernised notions around emotional well-being and therapeutic mental health services may be alienating to those whose responses to their experience of abuse are understandably confused or angry or who do not understand the context of mental health provision in the UK. As one separated young person from Africa explained:

> It's different here . . . everything when you say you are stressed, they going to say you are mental . . . something like that . . . I don't like someone to call me mental. Mental is one who become like crazy or can't think, who fight if you move close . . . this is the one we call mental. Even like counselling, they may think I'm mental. That's why I don't like to use those types of services because I don't want anyone to say I'm mental . . . 'cos I don't think I'm mental.
>
> (quoted in Chase *et al.* 2008: 3)

Work undertaken by Kohli and Mitchell (2007) on separated children and young people identifies similar needs to those noted by Chase *et al.* (2008). In particular, it addresses the complex challenges for social work practice in trying to provide culturally sensitive services for children and young people.

While existing studies shed some light on the scope of trafficking of children and young people in the UK, they are unlikely to paint an exhaustive picture of the complex issues raised above. As noted within the scoping report undertaken by CEOP (2007), identification of cases improves as practitioners and the general public become more aware of the issues and more able to identify indicators of trafficking cases. Monitoring and analysis of child trafficking has been, and remains, challenging because of the fluid and clandestine nature of the crime (Sillen and Beddoe 2007).

Three further gaps have been identified:

- The backgrounds and context from which the children and young people arrive need to be better understood through research into the source countries, their efforts to prevent trafficking, and their relationship with other countries that might be involved during the transit of the child or young person. Accurate and reliable country of origin information that relates specifically to trafficking, or the trafficking of young people, is scarce and disparate.
- The young person's own account of why and how they were trafficked into the UK from abroad and the impact this has had on their development has not been researched. There has been no comprehensive review of young people's own accounts to date. Although there are serious ethical considerations that need to be borne in mind when planning such research, it is essential that a better, child-centred account of the reasons for, and experience of, trafficking is provided by the young people themselves.
- Finally, little is known about the problems faced by practitioners who are trying to recognise and respond to the needs of trafficked young people. It is this gap that this book begins to identify.

Conclusion

This chapter has provided an overview of some of the existing literature and policy frameworks that inform our understanding of trafficking. Despite the apparent clarity in policy strategies defining who should intervene, how, when and where, there remain difficulties in quantifying numbers of young people who have been trafficked into, within and out of the UK for the different forms of exploitation, resulting from poor awareness of indicators of trafficking and insufficient knowledge of associated child protection needs (Bokhari 2008).

Existing research, corroborated by findings from the research outlined in this book, reveals a need for specific resources to train and support practitioners who are safeguarding the full range of trafficked children and young people from abuse. Lord Laming (2009) recommended that social work be organised through social work units where an experienced social work consultant is supported in managing the more complex and emotionally demanding child protection cases. He also advocated that Children's Trusts ensure that a named and preferably co-located representative from the police, a community paediatric specialist and health visitors are active partners within each children's social work department. These recommendations were timely as many practitioners in our research noted the need for further training, for better support for multi-agency work and for designated senior staff to lead the interventions in relation to the complex trafficking cases. The Munro review also advocates a clearer focus on the relationship between the children's service provider and the children on their case load, noting that it is through good relationships that children learn to model new ways of relating with adults, and understand that not all relationships need to be abusive or harmful (Munro, 2011).

However, recent funding cuts to local authorities and charities working with young people undermine these laudable aims. The 'localism' agenda where the 'big society' is the source for intervention leaves little scope for meeting the often hidden needs of trafficked children. In addition, there is increased worry that as funding becomes scarcer, services for trafficked young people will be reduced. Just one example of central government cuts within the last two years is of the abolition of Home Office funding for the NSPCC CTAIL. This has left the service dependent on voluntary contributions and charitable funding.

There remains a worrying assumption that the term 'children' embraces all needs and that the particular circumstances of young people do not need to be separated from those of younger children. The next chapter explores how the research aimed to gain an understanding of practitioners' views of trafficked young people and of the resources they needed to support their interventions.

3 Researching practitioners' responses to trafficked young people

Methods, ethics and governance

This chapter explains the rationale for the research which informs the content of this book. The research took place between 2007 and 2009 but was preceded by 18 months of preparation and fundraising and has been followed by dissemination and training events. In view of that, while the book draws on findings from the specific research, it also considers the continuing context for work with trafficked children and young people. In this chapter we set out the aims of the research and the procedures we followed for establishing quality assurance and governance and for ensuring that ethical issues were addressed. The chapter looks at how and why specific sites were selected for the research, and explains how the research was conducted and analysed. In conclusion, it looks at some of the limitations on undertaking research on this topic, placing the research in political and historical context to consider the boundaries created by resource limitations.

The origin of the research

Throughout the late 1990s and early 2000s there was growing concern that the increased movement of people between and within countries in the developing 'globalised' economy was bringing with it opportunities for the expansion of informal economies such as trafficking in drugs and people. In particular, there was concern that the number of young people being trafficked into the UK for different forms of exploitation was increasing. During the same period, there was extensive tightening of immigration and asylum policies within the UK and across Europe (Castles 2002).

Simultaneously with these growing restrictions on migration, the UK Human Trafficking Centre and the Child Exploitation Online Protection Agency, both police-led agencies, were formed. These police agencies, and NGOs such as Stop the Traffick, ECPAT, the NSPCC Child Trafficking Information Line and the Anti-Slavery Alliance were beginning to raise awareness of the needs of children and young people trafficked into the UK from abroad. As noted, while the DCSF (2007) guidance on safeguarding trafficked children and young people provided some frameworks for practitioners in the field to follow, it failed to distinguish between problems relating to younger trafficked children and those relating to older adolescents. Agencies affiliated with the National Working Group for Sexually Exploited Children and Young People (NWG), an umbrella organization supporting a network of projects working across the UK with sexually exploited young people, were increasingly concerned about young people's disclosure of being trafficked into and/or within the UK. This work identified a need for an in-depth study to explore how, when and why practitioners were identifying young people as trafficked, what resources they were using to work with the trafficked young person and what problems they were experiencing in accessing and using the resources.

Before looking in detail at the specific research aims, it is helpful to clarify two features. First, the focus of the research was on providing qualitative data from interviews and focus groups with practitioners about their work with trafficked young people. It was already established that the identification and recording of cases of trafficking was, and today continues to be, inadequate (CEOP 2007, 2009; ECPAT UK 2007, 2011a), so that the methods were designed to find out why this might be and what practitioners thought might help to remedy the problems identified. The research was not designed to create reliable quantitative data about the numbers of young people trafficked into the UK.

Secondly, the research continued to look at the questions and tensions within definitions of 'internal' and 'international' trafficking. While the focus of the research was directed towards the complexities facing practitioners in identifying and responding to young people trafficked from abroad, it also considered some of the issues arising from casework with 'internal' or 'domestic' trafficking of UK nationals (see chapter 2 for more details on this). While the overarching aim of the research was to draw on practitioners' experiences to provide a qualitative analysis of the identification of and work with young people trafficked from abroad, the different interpretations of the meaning of 'trafficking' were explored.

The particular aims of the research were to

- identify three appropriately positioned localities within which in-depth research with practitioners could take place;
- explore in depth the different ways in which 'trafficking' is understood by a range of practitioners from different service agencies in the three locations and provide evidenced recommendations for practice in their areas;
- consider the obstacles that might emerge in identifying the numbers of young people trafficked in the three localities;

- chart the trajectory of the trafficked young person following identification and through the process of accessing support services, noting how the first and subsequent points of contact were managed;
- undertake, where possible, documentary case study analysis to provide a profile of young people identified in each locality, including age, nationality, country of origin, the reason they were trafficked into the country and a summary of their current circumstances;
- discover how different practitioners understood the immediate and longer term needs of the young people concerned;
- identify how the professionals feel these needs would be best met.

Staffing, governance and dissemination of the research

Following agreement of the specific aims outlined above, the research was commissioned by the NSPCC to take place in partnership with the University of Bedfordshire, Institute for Applied Social Research. Part of the funding for the work came from a donation to the NSPCC by The Children's Charity. In addition, the NSPCC and the University of Bedfordshire contributed to overheads and staff costs. In this way, although the main funding was from an independent donor, both sides of the partnership agreement contributed financially to the research.

The research team referred to an independent academic adviser and reported through written and verbal presentations to a multi-agency advisory group which met quarterly throughout the duration of the research. The research advisory group was comprised of a representative from the safeguarding team of each of the three research sites. These staff were responsible for supporting the research team with each site. The findings from the research were collated into a draft report which was circulated among members of the advisory group for comment and amended prior to publication. The final research report was launched at a national conference organised through Making Research Count (a national research dissemination network whose membership includes children and young people's services, adult and community care departments, health trusts and independent sector organizations) and is available on the NSPCC and University of Bedfordshire websites. This book, co-authored by the research team, was an agreed form of dissemination of the research findings.

Ethical considerations and confidentiality

Ethical approval for the research project was given by the University of Bedfordshire, School of Applied Social Studies Ethics Committee, and by the NSPCC Research Ethics Committee. Scrutiny of all ethical considerations followed points identified in the World Health Organization publication *WHO Ethical and Safety Recommendations for Interviewing Trafficked Women* (Zimmerman and Watts 2003); the ethical guidelines of the Economic and Social Research Council; and the British Sociological Association Ethical Guidelines. Preparations for ethical approval also followed guidelines produced by Barnardo's for research with children and young people.

It was agreed that the three sites where the research took place would not be identified. The names of agencies and the practitioners involved in the research would also remain anonymous. Where relevant, data would reveal the type of agency involved (such as voluntary organisation, health service provider, statutory social work provider) but no other details would be given regarding staff names or the departments they represented. Recognising that the research aimed to reveal the complexities confronted by a range of practitioners, it was agreed that practitioners were more likely to feel able to discuss the problems they faced if they were reassured there would be no personal recriminations. However, practitioners were informed in advance that if researchers identified practice that was felt to place children and young people at risk of significant harm (as defined in the Children Act 1989), the practitioner(s) involved would be informed that details of the concern were to be passed to the relevant site representative on the research advisory group. Practitioners' identities are hidden through a coding system whereby each interviewee is ascribed a number. The research team retained a record of the professional identity and site for each numbered practitioner. It was agreed by the research advisory group that it was not necessary to identify either site or profession of practitioners, since the purpose was to gain an overall impression of the experiences as expressed by all agencies.

It was also decided that the research team would study case files of trafficked young people rather than directly interview young people themselves. The team, and advisory group, were aware that being 'interviewed' was a complex and potentially traumatic experience for young people who have been abused by strangers and subsequently interviewed by police, border controls and 'official' agencies relating to their status. It was considered that the young person might well be fearful of the status of the research interview, being concerned that the interview might be linked to questions of residence and citizenship. In addition, compliance with good practice and ethical concerns means that an interview with a trafficked young person should only be carried out through access via gatekeepers. There was concern that asking young people more questions about their circumstances might upset an ongoing programme of work developed with the gatekeeper. In addition, an interpreter might need to be employed. It is recognised that there is limited availability of skilled and experienced interpreters (see chapter 7 for more detail on this), so this was an additional barrier to interviewing young people directly. The researcher might have needed to bring a different interpreter than the one hitherto used for practice interventions with the young person, and that would have raised questions about the number of different people the young person was asked to discuss their circumstances with. If the interpreter represented the community responsible for the abuse experienced, the young person might have felt threatened or, alternatively, embarrassed that someone from their own country or community knew of the traumas they had undergone.

With all these points in mind, it was confirmed that the focus of the work should be on practitioners' experiences of working with trafficked young people. However, it was agreed that the three sites would be asked to provide case files of trafficked children they had worked with. The files were to be anonymised and then analysed to identify times and levels of intervention and to explore patterns emerging in practice.

The identity of children and young people was protected through the use of pseudonyms. The examples of case material that are used in discussions of findings for the work are composites, drawing on different sections of the analysis of the actual case studies. Composite case studies were created by the research team and circulated to the advisory group for consideration before publication of the final research report. Each composite case study was given a code for use in publications. There are no case studies in the research report or in this book that could be traced to any one individual young person's circumstances.

In addition to the considerations above, the ethical approval secured emotional support for the researchers, recognising that the emotional burden of listening to and reading about traumatic experiences of child abuse would have an impact on the researchers and their ability to maintain an objective review of the data. This point has been developed well by Melrose, who considers how ethics committees need to address the 'emotional labour' experienced by researchers who are researching sensitive topics. Drawing on her work as a researcher and experience of chairing ethics committees, she notes the need for ethics committees to be mindful of the need to protect children and researchers from harm without also using 'sensitive' material as a reason for preventing research from taking place. Looking at how the 'ethics industry' has proliferated in recent years, she argues that the most marginalised, damaged and confrontational communities might be excluded from research data on the grounds that they were too 'dangerous' or 'hard to reach' and on the grounds of 'protecting' researchers' well-being. While she advocates for ethics committees to be mindful of the need to safeguard the physical and emotional well-being of both researchers and researched, she also refutes the rejection of 'difficult' research for fear that marginalised communities might become, by default, further marginalised in, if not indeed excluded from emerging research data and, consequently, the ways we understand the social world (Melrose 2011).

We were mindful of these important potential contradictions explored by Melrose and, subsequent to completing the research, we have argued that a comprehensive piece of work needs to take place to engage with trafficked young people themselves, represent their choices directly and look at the scope for empowerment of trafficked young people through the process of engaging with participatory action research. This aim is still waiting to be realised!

The sites for the research

Three sites were chosen to provide insight into different policy contexts and to reflect different densities of caseloads arising from geographical, demographic and environmental variations. Two sites closer to airports received more referrals of young people trafficked into the UK from abroad than the site positioned away from an air or sea port, where referrals tended to be mainly of UK citizens trafficked for sexual exploitation. This affected practitioners' understandings of trafficking, with those from sites near airports considering trafficking only in terms of trafficking into the UK from abroad, and those from the site further from airports tending to define trafficking as involving young people born within the UK for the purpose of sexual exploitation. The three sites were asked to identify their current data recording and monitoring processes around cases of trafficking of young people. In the main, these data were not available. The closest data that were available were from records of unaccompanied asylum-seeking children. Sites were asked to explain their local procedures and to note the agencies they involved in working with separated and trafficked young people.

Research methods

Three different research methods were used to explore the research questions. Focus groups were run in each site; semi-structured interviews were undertaken; and 37 case studies of trafficked young people were studied.

The research questions were piloted first through pilot interviews with colleagues from within the NSPCC and, secondly, through an initial focus group in one of the three sites.

The team then ran focus groups with practitioners from a range of disciplines in each of the three sites. These were followed by one-to-one semi-structured interviews with practitioners who had specific experience, interest or expertise in practice issues emerging from work with trafficked young people. With agreement from the practitioners, the interviews were digitally recorded. The recordings were transcribed and analysed thematically through use of NVivo software. Finally, the three sites identified case files representing details of young people who had been trafficked. Findings were analysed thematically using both manual analysis undertaken by each of the three researchers and through use of NVivo software. The findings from each of the three methods were triangulated to identify any reoccurring and interconnected themes.

The focus groups

A total of 65 practitioners took part in a total of nine focus groups: three focus groups run in each of the three sites. Two researchers were present at each focus group and the focus group discussion was digitally recorded, permission having been granted by those present. Focus group discussion followed a list of topics framed around the generic research questions. The size of the focus group varied depending upon practitioner availability and expertise in each of the three sites. No focus group was smaller than five or larger than ten people (see Appendix, table 1, for the numbers of practitioners attending focus groups in each of the three sites and the numbers of trafficked children and young people they had worked with).

Focus group members were given written documentation about the research project in advance, outlining the key research questions. The transcribed recordings from the focus groups were analysed manually by two separate members of the research team. The data were analysed thematically and the findings cross-referenced between the two staff members. A summary of the thematic analysis was presented to the research project advisory group for comments and review.

One-to-one semi-structured interviews

One-to-one semi-structured interviews were carried out with 72 practitioners from each of the three sites. Purposeful sampling took place to interview practitioners who had attended focus groups and noted specific experience in working with trafficked young people. This identified 65 practitioners from the focus groups. Seven further practitioners were interviewed who had not been able to attend focus groups but who were recommended as having specific experience or expertise in the field. See Appendix, table 2, for the professional status of practitioners in focus groups and interviews.

The semi-structured interviews followed a set format of questioning developed from the generic research questions. The questions were piloted with colleagues from the NSPCC and the University of Bedfordshire. They were amended following piloting. With agreement from the practitioner, the interviews were digitally recorded. The recordings were transcribed and analysed thematically through use of NVivo software.

Case studies

Finally, the data recorded within case files pertaining to 37 young people were studied using a case study template. The template was piloted with NSPCC practitioners from CTAIL and with members of the CTAIL young people's advisory group. The final template used reflected amendments recommended following this piloting exercise.

A minimum of five case studies were sought from each area. The information from case study files was manually placed on the case study template by the research staff and input into NVivo software for thematic analysis. The quantitative data from the case studies are outlined below, while qualitative data are incorporated within the body of the report in chapters 3 to 6. (See Appendix, table 3, for details of the case studies analysed; table 4 for the gender and age breakdown of the 37 case studies analysed; table 5 for reasons for trafficking in the 37 case studies analysed; and table 6 giving details of the country of origin of the children and young people in the 37 cases studied.) It is important to note that of the 37 cases, 18 were of situations where the young person was reported missing or had experienced periods of going missing from care.

Processes for dealing with trafficked children in each site

One of the first tasks of the research was to establish how, when and where each site identified trafficked young people. Following enquires it transpired that, in the main, this was through services working with sexually exploited children and young people.

In Site 1, the LSCB procedures for safeguarding trafficked young people were used and a referral and assessment service conducted as an enquiry jointly with the police (child abuse investigation team) under section 47 of the 1989 Children Act and/or the Airport Intelligence Unit. Where cases included alleged sexual exploitation, a formal strategy meeting was held and a safeguarding plan was devised as part of the strategy. As sexual abuse is a category of abuse under *Working Together to Safeguard Children* (DCSF 2006), it would necessitate a child protection plan. This plan was integrated into the care plan if the young person became looked-after. If the young person remained in the community, the referral and assessment team or the child in need team would hold the case, making sure that the child protection plan was not discontinued until the risk of sexual exploitation had been removed. These child protection plans were monitored by an independent reviewing officer, who would chair the child protection conferences relating to the case.

In addition, this site had an Airport Protocol, which covered issues relating to child trafficking. This protocol specifically addressed the site's unique situation as a port of entry. It had a virtual 'airport intake team'. The referral and assessment team dealt with all cases of sexual exploitation, including those who were UASC.

In Site 2, the Children Quality Assurance Unit followed the review system for looked-after children, identifying cases of sexual exploitation and trafficking within this review. The local authority had a Sexual Exploitation Project which took referrals from professionals, parents/carers and children. All children who met the referral criteria were the subject of a strategy planning meeting under the Site 2 Protocol for safeguarding trafficked children and young people. There was also ongoing planning guided by this protocol for children found to be at risk of sexual exploitation. Specific allegations of abuse were investigated by the children's services assessment service, together with the police. A sexual exploitation personal adviser was appointed to work with young people who were found to be trafficked for sexual exploitation. There was an additional specific protocol for managing child protection issues for the Unaccompanied Minors Service, the Asylum Screening Unit and the police.

In Site 3, young people trafficked for sexual exploitation were referred to the sexual exploitation service, a multi-agency partnership between the safeguarding children service, police and a team of youth workers and staff from the local drug and alcohol project. An individual strategy meeting was held about each young person and reviewed on a regular basis until the young person was 18 or until they were thought to be no longer at risk. For any cases that did not apparently involve sexual exploitation, the site had a referrals manual and a short protocol on child trafficking that explained the procedure to be used following identification. This involved developing a care plan and allocating a specific key worker to oversee implementation of the plan.

Recording and monitoring of trafficking cases in each site

In Site 1, the education and children's services used electronic recording where possible. If a young person was trafficked, details would be recorded on the case notes of the child. The indicators and reasons for this judgement would be identified as part of the care plan/safeguarding /child protection plan. Each young person had a separate individual case file, held in the archives of the Council. No separate recording of child trafficking was kept, other than on individual case files. Site 1 did keep a separate record of children and young people who went missing. This was reported to the Safeguarding Board on a quarterly basis in the form of a manual spreadsheet, held in the Safeguarding Children and Quality Assurance Service. There were situations where a young person was assessed as having been trafficked where they wouldn't have an active care plan but might have a safeguarding plan. This would be drawn up at the strategy meeting and detail issues that needed to be considered when developing the care plan. The safeguarding plan is similar to the child protection plan but not reviewed at child protection conferences by the independent reviewing officers.

In Site 2, data on trafficking were held by the Children's Quality Assurance Unit. The sexual exploitation database also recorded data of suspected trafficking cases.

In Site 3, suspected cases of a trafficked child or young person were monitored by the asylum team.

In the absence of a central database, it was difficult to ascertain the number of incidents of trafficking of young people. Also, as this research project shows, the identification of a trafficked young person depends on the levels of awareness and expertise of the practitioner or carer concerned. This means that cases of suspected trafficking may be identified in one situation and overlooked in another. In addition, the sites varied as to whether they included the movement of UK nationals within the UK in the definition of trafficked young people. These combined factors meant that the data available to reveal the scale of the problem were, in the main, unreliable.

Recording and managing missing children in each site

It is widely recognised that children who are trafficked invariably 'go missing' and are abducted from or run away from their allocated place of safety (see chapter 2). Worryingly, research shows some cases of 'going missing' that have resulted from inappropriate placements being allocated, with the location and nature of the 'home' provided to the child adding to, rather than protecting from, the risks of further trafficking (ECPAT UK 2010). The strategies employed by the sites to prevent going missing were therefore of significance.

Site 1 followed local city-wide guidance on Safeguarding Children Missing from Care and Home. A total of 89 young people left local authority accommodation without leaving a forwarding address between 1 January 2006 and 31 December 2008. These young people had all arrived through the airport and were under immigration controls. The majority went missing within seven days of arrival at the airport. All of them were between the ages of 16 and 18, although their precise ages were not clear as they had not been age assessed. The majority (53) were Chinese, Mandarin-speaking females. All of them were reported missing to the police, UKBA and port authorities, and received a formal safeguarding response using child protection procedures. The trends around missing children were monitored by the LSCB trafficking and exploitation subgroup, and reported quarterly to the LSCB main board meeting. An agreement had been reached with UKHTC and UK BA that they would receive all intelligence and data around missing children from Site 1. This fed into any national law operations being run by the Serious Organised Crime Agency. Such arrangements have now been formalised within the National Referral Mechanism, whereby all data on suspected and actual trafficked cases are referred to the UKHTC and to UKBA.

All young people arriving at the airport in Site 1 were given a leaflet about the dangers of going missing, and the risks of child trafficking. This leaflet was in Mandarin and English, and was translated into other languages to fit the profile of separated children in Site 1. These leaflets were also used by the Red Cross to forewarn young people of the risk of trafficking while they were in transition to the UK. Several children and young people have returned to care in Site 1, after first going missing from the airport.

Site 2 had recently developed a focus on preventing children and young people from going missing by providing a particular body of work in collaboration with police and other services targeted at the child or young person at the point of arrival into the country. As a result, the numbers of separated young people who went missing from care without leaving a forwarding address dropped dramatically. Data on children and young people going missing were limited as there were discrepancies in how long young people were thought to be missing for and there were a large number of repeats, when the same child or young person went missing on more than one occasion. The missing children's worker saw approximately 280 children per year who went missing and then returned to the authority. However, the majority of children who were thought to have been trafficked were UK citizens trafficked internally within the UK. The borough had extensive missing from care and home procedures which required a swift multi-agency response to any case identified. It was noted that it is rare (one or two cases) for a child or young person under the age of 16 to go missing permanently.

Children who went missing from Site 3 were immediately subjected to 'tracking' though the site's current protocol guiding multi-agency work for missing young people. As most of the young people recorded as trafficked had experienced internal trafficking for the purpose of sexual exploitation, the sexual exploitation service maintained regular contact between the key worker and the allocated child protection worker at the site.

Summary of findings from the local sites

The initial overview of data available from the sites in recording cases of trafficking of young people illustrated the many problems in identifying the young people concerned and then mainlining accurate and transparent records of their progress. As noted throughout the research, there is little reliable evidence recorded of data on trafficked children and young people or on those who go missing.

In the sites under study, we found only a small number of recorded cases of child trafficking. This might highlight a gap in recording suspected (as opposed to confirmed) cases of child trafficking rather than an absence of trafficked children per se in these areas. Site 1, for instance, reported a substantial number of children who had gone missing and where it was suspected they had been trafficked. These children were recorded as 'missing' rather than as 'victims of being trafficked'. In Site 2, trafficking was most likely to be recorded on the Children's Quality Assurance Unit's database on sexual exploitation, constituting one category among many other risk factors and indicators; and in Site 3, cases of trafficked children had been monitored through police investigations of cases of child trafficking as a crime. As such, it was unclear how many cases of trafficked children and young people go unnoticed and how many suspected cases of child trafficking are dropped due to lack of evidence or are never fully investigated.

Overall it was surmised that, in the main, the issue of trafficking appeared to have fallen towards sexual exploitation services.

Conclusions and limitations to the work

This chapter has explored how the research data were collated and analysed and has given an overview of the three sites where the research took place. As outlined in chapter 2, the validity of estimates of the total number of children and young people affected by trafficking has been questioned. Analysis of the recording systems within specific sites illustrates some of the problems in recording these data and in collating them in a way that can be useful in informing practice. It has been argued that the development and use of the National Referral Mechanism has exacerbated rather than smoothed some of the conflicts between immigration and child protection services, particularly around when and why a trafficked child should be identified, with many cases of child trafficking not being identified or recorded with shared consistency of meaning. This has led to piecemeal and partial data (see Anti-Trafficking Monitoring Group 2012 and chapter 2 for further details on this).

The chapter also illustrates how many practitioners work with a range of different levels of understanding of trafficking, often due to geographical location and proximity to airports or points of entry to the UK. It explains how and why some understandings of trafficking are influenced by agendas seeking to prevent child sexual exploitation and to prevent the 'going missing' of children and young people. In all, this chapter has shown the complex realities facing many local authorities who are working to prevent trafficking and to address the damage that it causes to young people.

The book turns now to look in more detail at some of the findings from the research, focusing specifically on practitioners' responses to cases of trafficked young people that they describe and on the case studies analysed in the research.

4 Trafficking as a process, not a one-off event

In previous chapters we have outlined how the trafficking of children and young people is child abuse and argued that only a child-centred system of child protection is suitable as a means of intervention to support the young person. We have also explored the policy context that has led to the development of guidance for supporting trafficked children and young people, showing how the identification of a young person as trafficked is the first step to providing adequate protection.

In this chapter we highlight a key finding of our research – that trafficking is a process occurring over the longer term, rather than being a one-off, and sometimes nationally bounded event in the life of a young person. It is argued that from this understanding of trafficking as a process a number of factors unfold: the identification of a trafficked young person needs to be understood as a process, rather than identification relying on a one-off disclosure; and recovery will be a lengthy process, requiring adequate resources over a period of time.

As discussed in previous chapters, trafficking invariably incorporates physical and emotional abuse, neglect and, often, sexual abuse. These forms of abuse and control mechanisms are incorporated into the life of a young person and, as such, may be integrated into their lives before their arrival in the UK and during their time within the UK or pre-departure from the UK. The trafficking experiences can be 'hidden' within the day-to-day activities of a young person, making the task of identifying a trafficked young person difficult. We look at how an understanding of these dynamics, many of which occur beyond the national boundaries of the UK, is an essential component of understanding the multiple forms of trafficking of young people.

This process of trafficking is explored and illustrated through a series of composite, anonymous case studies drawn from interviews and focus groups (see chapter 3 for details of the research methods used). The views and observations of practitioners who were working closely with trafficked young people are outlined to show how trafficking is understood, how our knowledge of trafficking has been enhanced through the experience of practitioners and how limits to our understanding can be exploited by traffickers.

Young people affected by trafficking in the UK

In chapter 2 we noted that the trafficking of young people into, within and out of the country has become an increasingly important and debated issue in the academic (Craig *et al.* 2007; Bokhari 2008, 2009), voluntary (ECPAT UK 2007, 2009b) and statutory (CEOP 2007, 2009) sectors.

As Bovarnick (2010) has succinctly suggested, practitioners within the voluntary and statutory sectors in the UK currently hold differing defini-tions of trafficking which have an impact on the ways young people are identified and responded to. We have already noted how UK debates around the trafficking of young people are framed within debates on immigration and asylum, with systems set up to control migration on the one hand, and child protection concerns on the other. In recent years a third dynamic, that of young offending might be added to this framing, with accounts of young people being placed in youth offending institutions after experiencing coer-cive and exploitative working conditions in the UK.

These forms of abuse and mechanisms of control are incorporated into the day-to-day lives of young people. Where international cases of trafficking are concerned, abuse and control are integrated into young people's lives before arrival into the UK. For both 'internal' and 'international' cases, abuse and control continues during their lives within the UK and may, in some cases, continue after departure from the country. It is these 'global points of vulnerability' (Hynes 2010a) that we want to focus on here, noting that this entails an understanding of dynamics that occur beyond the national boundaries of the UK, an essential component of understanding the traffick-ing of young people in its multitude of forms.

GLOBAL POINTS OF 'VULNERABILITY'

Case study: Yu Chan's story

Prior to arriving in the UK, Yu Chan was, at the age of 14, trafficked from China to Europe, where she was forced to engage in sex work. She had left an impoverished community in China, having been brought up in an orphanage after her mother died in childbirth and there being no knowledge of the whereabouts of her father.

In the UK, Yu Chan presented to Children's Services aged 15 after escaping from a brothel. At the time she was five months pregnant. She was initially placed in local authority care but a number of placement breakdowns were precipitated when she went missing for periods of time.Three days after giving birth, Yu Chan again went missing, this time with her baby.

A few days later, Yu Chan telephoned her keyworker and informed her that she had sent her baby back to China. It later emerged that the baby might have been sent to the same orphanage from which Yu Chan had been trafficked. Professionals also thought that she had little understanding of the benefits and support to which she was entitled to help her keep her baby in the UK, partly as a result of a lack of appropriate interpretation services in her interviews. Some reports suggested she had undiagnosed learning difficulties, defining her as naive. Practitioners also felt that she was subject to pressures by unknown people, particularly from her own 'community'.

It was later revealed that she had been threatened by her traffickers, who said that she owed them money and that the baby could repay the debt. She was threatened with her own and her baby's death if the debt was not repaid. Suspicions that someone might be controlling her and that she might be linked to organised crime in some way were discussed in strategy meetings within the local authority. However, the way in which money, tickets and necessary documentation were found for her baby to be sent back to China remained unclear.

When Yu Chan subsequently fell pregnant again, tight interventions were put in place to monitor her and her newborn baby.

The process of trafficking

Yu Chan's case clearly illustrates how the trafficking of a young person can begin in one country, continue through potentially a variety of other countries, and extend throughout the young person's lifespan. Yu Chan had been raised in an orphanage and had little knowledge of and no contact with her own family members. For Yu Chan, there was no one event where exploitation and maltreatment began or ended. She also did not have a thorough understanding of where she was within the UK, of what legislation was there to protect her, or of her entitlement to support. Foster carers who had tried to support her were frustrated by her pattern of going missing, a pattern orchestrated by the traffickers who were abusing her. Her exploitation and the pattern of abuse she had experienced were then extended into the next generation with the process of trafficking and exploitation continuing when traffickers took her child.

Yu Chan's experience demonstrates how trafficking can be 'hidden' in the day-to-day activities of young people, making identification difficult. On becoming pregnant with her second child, Yu Chan was ultimately identified as a trafficked child herself. However, what became clear over time was how the abuse had continued throughout her life and, potentially, led to abuse into the next generation.

The idea that an episode of trafficking is a short cycle in which a young person is 'kidnapped', trafficked and then 'rescued' only applied to a minority of cases. Rather, the experiences of trafficking portrayed in case files suggested a much longer term process, embedded in the socio-economic and political contexts and circumstances of abuse that particular children found themselves in at any given point in time.

This type of trafficking is inextricably linked to both globalisation and the promotion and protection of human rights. Dynamics of social exclusion and inclusion that result from inequalities within the global economy and ongoing conflicts around the world create situations whereby young people can be separated from their families. It is in this global context that 'vulnerabilities' need to be explored.

Identification of a child or young person is also a process, not a one-off event

The experiences of many trafficked young people need to be understood in terms of the way circumstances in the UK differ from countries of origin and from countries through which the young person may have travelled. Kunz (1973) drew attention to the idea that migrations have different 'vintages', with each 'vintage' having its own set of circumstances which are therefore different from those of previous or subsequent migrations. For young people who are trafficked, individual circumstances may be extremely varied, something which adds to the complexity of this phenomenon for practitioners working with them.

The significant impact that a different country of origin will have on the trafficked young person's experience is beginning to be recognised in UK debates about trafficking. However, observations by the practitioners about emerging 'trends' tended to be based solely on individual cases encountered, rather than informed by authoritative country-of-origin reports or reliable sources (Pearce *et al.*2009). As one practitioner commented: 'What we find is that there tends to be particular nationalities who gravitate towards particular types of work or are trafficked for particular types of purposes' (CS007).

If more accurate and reliable knowledge were available to practitioners about the young person's country of origin, including information about civil, political or socio-economic human rights issues, they would be better informed and would have a more realistic recognition of the situations experienced by the young person they were working with. They would understand better why the young person might have moved. Understanding the reasons behind these different migrations trajectories for trafficked young people is an area yet to be fully explored. While 'vintages' of a particular nationality may share some atavistic qualities with previous arrivals, there is a danger that informal 'profiling' of nationalities may lead to dangerous stereotyping. This may pose a barrier to accommodating the full range of possible reasons why a young person has been trafficked and, potentially, reduce the possibility of identifying a young person as trafficked.

The mechanisms through which trafficking abuses are perpetrated are incorporated into the overall process of migration. They are integrated into the young person's life and it is essential that trafficking is understood in this way. For international cases, the initial impetus may emanate from the circumstances of the family, who may or may not have an understanding of the potentially abusive structures inherent in the process of smuggling or trafficking. Young people who have been trafficked may arrive from a range of situations of socio-economic deprivation, extreme poverty, social exclusion, discrimination, international or civil war or of persecution within their countries of origin. The element of exploitation may remain hidden until after they are away from their country of origin. As seen above in the case of Yu Chan, exploitation may continue through their life and into the next generation.

For cases of 'internal' or 'domestic' trafficking, similar processes may be present. Although the young person is not crossing international borders and therefore not having to negotiate the additional barriers of language and culture, abuse and/or coercion may have been experienced in earlier childhood and may still be ongoing into adulthood. Disclosure of child sexual abuse is largely silent, about what is often a witness-free crime that is actively hidden by perpetrators. Disclosure of child sexual abuse is also a process that occurs over time, sometimes well into adulthood. Retrospective studies of adults suggest factors such as the relationship to the perpetrator, age at first incident of abuse, use of physical force, severity of abuse, and demographic variables such as gender and ethnicity have an impact on a child's willingness to disclose abuse (Allnock 2010). The young person's capacity to speak out about their abuse may well depend on a number of factors, including how normalised their exploitation has been made to become. Likewise, if a young person has been coerced or forced into thinking that exploitation through trafficking is 'normal', they will not come forward to identify it as a problem in need of remedy.

Recovery from trafficking is a lengthy process

Regardless of country of origin, trafficking has a devastating impact on the young person. As noted, understanding that trafficking is a lengthy process taking place possibly throughout a young person's lifespan means appreciating that any recovery plan is also necessarily a lengthy process. Recognising the adolescent's need to become autonomous, self-directed and self-determined, this will mean allowing time for rebuilding a young person's sense of agency within a care plan, looking at the role they can play in securing their own safety without placing the entire onus on them. This is a careful balance of power sharing to be initiated by practitioners, who on the one hand are protecting the young person from abuse, and on the other hand helping them to develop as autonomous individuals and potential adults. It means supporting them through a recognition of their victim status into managing their own agency. In essence, this means that the young person needs first to have acknowledged that they have been a victim, something many young people are understandably averse to doing. As one practitioner noted, one young man had argued strongly against the imposition of a 'victim' label: 'I might be abused, but I am not dead!' (Interview 007). This young man felt that he would have died if he had not left his country of origin, having witnessed the murder of his father and having lost contact with his mother and brother.

The complex mix of vulnerabilities and resilience that are demonstrated by any child are another factor in the identification of a young person as trafficked (Boyden and Hart 2007; Hart and Tyrer 2006; Hynes 2010b). Overcoming adversity, while building resilience, does not endow superhuman powers. The previous vulnerabilities will remain and, despite appearing strong in one situation, the young person may suddenly become fearful and vulnerable in another situation. In other words, a trafficked child may be resilient to one risk but not to another and professionals need to bear this in mind when considering the safety of a child. A trafficked child may also not wish to conform to any 'victim' image held by professionals. Despite this, it is important that practitioners do not collude with the young person's apparent resilience, noting that their vulnerability to exploitation may be hidden but very much there under the surface in their day-to-day lives. One way for young people to hide from the reality of the horrific experiences they have had is to 'hide' away from anything that reminds them of trafficking, including rejecting acknowledgement of the term itself. Again, this was something that practitioners needed to be wary of. However, many practitioners themselves had different understandings of what they thought trafficking was. This often led to confused responses to a young person's process of disclosure and recovery.

Practitioners understanding of trafficking as a process or as a one-off event

Throughout the study that informs this book, there was a tangible level of confusion and uncertainty among many practitioners with regard to knowing and applying a definition of trafficking in their practice. The tendency was to perceive it as an event, a one-off incident of forced movement, rather than a process, a part of a continuum of abuse and neglect. The internationally agreed definition provided by the Palermo Protocol, replicated in the lists of risk indicators and protocols devised in the UK, was often unknown to professionals. For example, one practitioner who had considerable experience of dealing with trafficked children explained:

> I have looked at all the different definitions that they have and I realised that there isn't a full definition that everyone sticks to. It can be looked at very differently. I don't think that we have had a prescribed definition . . . it wasn't like, this is definitely it and this is definitely not. It was based on the individual.
>
> (Interview 25)

Another practitioner, with less experience and knowledge about trafficking issues, reiterated this: 'I suppose it's maybe because we are sometimes working to different definitions and that people don't really know what definitions we are working to' (Interview 21).

It was not uncommon for a young person to be identified as trafficked some years after their arrival and claiming asylum. However, this relied on the sensitivity of a practitioner to the possibility that trafficking occurred in the early part of the young person's trajectory and that it had been hidden over time. Appropriate training could aid recognition of the way that having been trafficked can be integrated into the young person's life. With this training, practitioners can become more familiar with the indicators for identifying trafficking and more open to recognising that some separated or unaccompanied asylum-seeking young people in their caseload may have been trafficked: 'It made me think a little bit more about whether all asylum-seeking children are trafficked . . . if it does include all of our asylum seekers then obviously I have got hundreds of names' (Interview 4).

When practitioners became better equipped to identify trafficking, they were more sensitive to understanding the mechanisms of exploitation, including the ways that young people might have been manipulated and abused. As one practitioner noted when talking of her definition of trafficking:

> Mine would be young people who were in some way forced or coerced or taken to this country for means such as prostitution or exploitation of

some sort. When I say taken, I don't always mean that they are forced into it or abducted. I mean that they could believe that they are coming in for a good reason but because they are young people they don't really understand what's happening. Maybe some form of blackmail, emotional blackmail from the traffickers to get young people to come over here because if they don't something might happen to their family.

(Interview 5)

This, and the range of definitions provided by practitioners, revealed the complexities experienced in trying to understand and define a trafficked young person (Bovarnick 2010). The research showed that, with training, practitioners were better able to understand the definition of child trafficking and to recognise that the identification of trafficking is a process of understanding the trajectories of an heterogeneous group, rather than an event occurring to particular clearly identified and compliant 'victims'.

The relationship between 'trafficking' and 'smuggling': implications for disclosure and intervention

Evidence from the research suggested that it was not always clear whether a separated young person had been 'trafficked' or 'smuggled', or whether practitioners felt that this distinction actually mattered in practice as the process of being trafficked might involve a conflation of the two. As outlined in chapter 2, distinctions between smuggling and trafficking can be easily blurred. To recap, smuggling involves moving a person across a border illegally and is a violation of state sovereignty, whereas trafficking involves the exploitation of a human being for financial gain or other benefits and is a violation of that person's human right to freedom. Force, coercion, deception and being misled are key aspects of the latter. While smuggling involves facilitating the transportation of an individual with their consent, trafficking involves a person being exploited by the trafficker as a commodity. Any initial consent to being smuggled can be invalidated by use of coercive or deceptive means and, definitionally, in the case of young people under the age of 18, consent is always irrelevant (Save the Children 2007).

The question of whether a young person was seen to be consenting to being smuggled was often confused in practitioners' minds, or diverted them from focusing on pursuing assessment of the extent of exploitation the young person might have experienced. As the distinction between experiences of trafficking and smuggling were blurred, there was a potential danger that a young person's journey might be classified as a case of smuggling rather than trafficking, with an assumption of the young person's active consent in their movement from place to place: 'I think it gets minimised when somebody labels a child as smuggled. . . . I think that it's almost as if they consider a smuggled child to be in on it. Whereas a trafficked child is being deceived all the way' (Interview 28).

If a young person is assumed to be 'in on it' rather than deceived, they can be blamed for 'running away' and can be assessed for return to the very location they may have been trying to, or forced to leave. While the practitioner above assumed a somewhat clear distinction between trafficking and smuggling, another noted that some cases which began as 'smuggling' changed to involve exploitaiton, therfore shifting to being classified as trafficking: 'We realised it wasn't always about sex trafficking . . . there were kids being used as domestics . . . people were bringing kids in under the wire, so smuggling them in but going on to exploit them here' (Interview 31).

The fact that some practitioners appeared confused about the distinction between smuggling and trafficking meant that the trafficking of the child was often hidden, or, in other situations, the child was sidelined into being identified as smuggled. While the actual process of the young person's movement may take different forms over a long period of time, and the exploitation they experience may intersect with different stages and times of their journey, this interchange between the two definitions was problematic when a young person was labelled as it undermined recognition of their exploitation. Practitioners' understandings of smuggling as involving someone who had not been forced to leave their country of origin sometimes meant that the exploitative character of relationships were not focused on. If a practitioner did not have enough evidence to consider a young person as trafficked, the potential dangers inherent in the misunderstanding had implications for their future. Any case for asylum may rest on the young person's experience of being trafficked and if this was not identified early enough a case for asylum would lack credibility.

However, some practitioners felt they had a clear understanding of the difference between the two:

> I think for a trafficked child, it's organised crime. I think that family members back home can be abused, the children can be threatened. I also don't think a child consents to being trafficked. A child, I guess, that is being smuggled, it's quite difficult I guess, because where they can be used interchangably. . . . But I would say smuggling is something that is maybe arranged by the family and it may be a safer route that's got some level of consent, that's just my understanding of it. I could be wrong. But I think that a trafficked child is much more worrying and they've been exploited, and are being exploited, and I think it's quite dangerous from, you know, the beginning to the end . . .
>
> (Interview 29)

The initial focus on trafficking as being about organised crime takes us directly back to the different perspectives on trafficking, be they human rights, migration management or organised crime perspectives. The question remains open as to whether a child can be smuggled without being exploited during the course of their movement and in their experiences at the point of destination. If, as suggested, the process of smuggling deprives them of their right to live and to integrate into a society, and as 'smuggling' remains part of the complex and often extremely dangerous process involved in escaping persecution, the practitioners needed to be assertive in ensuring that they helped the young person to identify and manage the impact of exploitation. Once identified, this exploitation needed to be recorded within the definition of the case as 'trafficking' so that data could accumulate about trafficked young people's experiences. To fail to do this, and to record an exploited child as one who was smuggled, not trafficked, would be to undermine any attempts to enhance the young person's long-term safety and well-being.

'Profiling' and 'othering' within the trafficking process

We have looked above at how practitioners benefit from training that helped them to understand the differences between a young person's experience of being trafficked and of being smuggled. With knowledge and experience, they became more attuned to recognising indicators of abuse within the long process of what the young person had undergone prior to, and during their time in the UK. As a result, more experienced practitioners recognised the potential for the process of trafficking to involve smuggling, but understood the significance in maintaining the dominant definition of trafficking. This would help to secure the young person their rights as outlined in the UNCRC, the Palermo Protocol and the DCSF guidance (2007).

In addition to this, practitioners who had worked with a number of cases and/or received sufficient training were extremely careful and cautious about making any generalised statements about the 'profiles' or 'trends' of the cases of trafficking they were dealing with. They recognised that during the process of being trafficked, simplistic and potentially damaging assumptions may be made both by traffickers and by child care and law enforcement professionals about the young person's background, culture and associated 'patterns' of abuse. This has been referred to as 'profiling' the young person. As one practitioner commented: 'profiling, yes, because (a), we don't like to profile, and (b), we don't want to seem [to think] that all Somalis bring in children for the purposes of benefit fraud because we don't believe that at all' (Interview 14).

Others were less careful to tread the delicate balance between identifying a trend in patterns of exploitation and labelling an entire 'community' as problematic: 'It seems to be that, I think it's quite prevalent in Somali families that it seems to be benefit fraud . . . so that's one conclusion we came to. I don't know about any of the others really' (Interview 6).

Some practitioners made very general statements and assumptions about cases from different continents: 'I've not dealt with anything from Africa at all but I get the impression that with African girls from some states there's much more of a tradition of selling them off as slaves effectively' (Interview 15). Or:

> I mean, one hears tales that the Chinese are linked to it more than anyone else, and brothels where you've girls who are literally chained in the basement to a radiator. I've certainly not seen anything of that nature with Eastern European girls which we've had.
>
> (Interview 15)

These views, gained from general assumptions about trafficking and source countries, were understandably and invariably based on encounters with a few cases of trafficking rather than a broader profile of evidence. In response to other research that has revealed similar concerns about assumed community profiles, it has been suggested that training in and the development of culturally competent child protection models would benefit practitioners (Korbin 2007). The specific concern here is that if one community is assumed to engage in one particular process of trafficking, assuming, for example, that one route for movement and one specific form of exploitation can be ascribed to one community or one source country, the range of different exploitative experiences and journeys remain hidden and undetected.

Through the problematic attribution of specific characteristics to a specific group of young people from one country of origin or community, it becomes possible to label them as an 'other'. This process of 'othering' involves the creation of 'difference' between one group and another (Castles and Davidson 2000: 44). By 'othering' the young person or the perpetrator abusing them, each are distanced from connection with the host community. The process of integration into and within communities that takes place to enable trafficking to occur is hidden. This is why 'othering' needs to be addressed as a problematic part of the trafficking discourse: it assumes somewhat simplistic and potentially limiting ways of seeing and understanding the complex forms of exploitation taking place.

Our research suggested that the particular vulnerabilities of 'internal' cases were more likely than those in cases of international trafficking to be recognised as part of a process of longer term abuse. Histories of abuse were often noted, as well as problems associated with the misuse of drugs and alcohol.

However, it was also found that practitioners involved in work with 'internal' trafficking cases (children born in the UK, exploited and trafficked) sometimes focused on perpetrators as being from populations from 'other' areas or countries beyond that of the local population. Assumptions about perpetrators were sometimes based on speculation or hearsay, and there was an undercurrent of placing the blame for some 'internal' trafficking on to perpetrators from outside the UK: 'I referred to them as Albanian but I think we had slightly more nationalities than that floating around . . . They were foreigners and they didn't have a very good command of English' (Interview 15).

Recent cases of prosecutions of abusers who have sexually exploited young people have fuelled assumptions that an external 'other' group of perpetrators are responsible for all sexual exploitation and internal trafficking (Pearce forthcoming). While the specific nature of individual cases cannot be disputed, and while all communities need to own responsibility for challenging and intervening in situations of abuse, the worry that 'othering' (in both internal and international trafficking discourses) can divert the lens away from some communities and encourage focus on others is significant. It can result in a denial that abusers come from all communities and that all young people can be at risk of trafficking. It somewhat halts an understanding of the lengthy process of exploitation as a complex process involving a range of interactions between and within communities and suggests that trafficking can be frozen as a one-off event orchestrated by one particular community. Among many of the worries about this is the concern that the processes of abuse taking place within families, care homes and immediate communities facing specific vulnerabilities caused by poverty and by previous abuse and neglect will be overlooked, and that trafficking, both internal within the UK and international, will be understood as something divorced from the vulnerabilities experienced by many, particularly those in local authority care, including residential care.

One particularly experienced practitioner speculated about this, noting that some specific groups of young people are vulnerable but assuming that it was only perpetrators from abroad who could identify and abuse this vulnerability. The abuser in this case is referred to as an 'other', someone from outside the UK: 'You have to wonder how people who come to this country can spot and pick out a child that is vulnerable so easily, and of course, why they can spot them and we can't' (Interview 11).

Chapter 2 clearly identified the purposes for the trafficking of young people. Traffickers may originate from the same community as such 'victims' of trafficking. This is as true for 'internal' or 'domestic' trafficking as it is for those trafficked across international borders. To simplify this into a problem caused by external others is to simplify and misrepresent the process of trafficking in the UK.

The importance of experience and knowledge in the identification process

---

Case study: Binta's story

Aged 16, Binta arrived in the UK in January 2007 from a region in an African country where extreme violations of human rights were a daily reality. Initially she was refused entry to the UK and an unsuccessful attempt was made to deport her the next day.

Children's Services saw her as a very mature and calm young woman who controlled her emotions extremely well given that it was suspected she had been through traumatic experiences. When initially interviewed she was anxious, gave hesitant answers and it was considered that she 'withheld' information about her immediate story.

When she first arrived, she lived with an 'aunt' after immigration had called her 'father' in her country of origin to clarify the address where she would be living. At this time the young woman denied that the man was her father and that the woman she would be living with was actually her aunt. Throughout, the 'aunt' was in possession of her papers, passport and documentation. She ran away from the 'aunt' and presented herself at Children's Services in another part of the country. Not believing her account, her return to her 'aunt' was facilitated, but she then admitted herself to a hospital with a virus. Health professionals became suspicious and she finally managed to obtain protection and was accommodated under section 20 of the Children Act 1989.

After five months working with her key worker, she disclosed that she thought she was coming to the UK for marriage. After another month of developing a positive working relationship, she disclosed some more details of how she had been trafficked. It was a full 12 months later that she disclosed details of rapes in her country of origin. By this time, her age meant that it was important to put together her case for asylum and, some 15 months later, detailed observation notes enabled her to be identified as 'trafficked'. The trafficking investigation needed to take priority over the asylum claim and her asylum interviews were therefore necessarily postponed.

Although described as 'bright' and 'capable', she was not able to attend formal education during this time. She did, however, register herself at a local library and worked through her GSCE coursework by herself in the hope of someday becoming a lawyer.

Trafficking and private fostering arrangements

As can be seen from Binta's case study, the process of identification can be lengthy. It took a full 15 months before enough detail was known by practitioners for her to be identified as having been trafficked. Practitioners did not feel that they were able to question the relationship status to the 'aunt' as a member of her extended family, although ultimately this turned out to not be the case. However, the detailed notes maintained on Binta's case by an experienced team ultimately allowed for an asylum claim based on the disclosures she had provided over the 15 months. This case study illustrates how informal or private fostering arrangements can sometimes hide the process used to traffic young people, and that trafficking does not always occur as a result of large-scale organised criminal networks.

Although not associated at the time with trafficking debates, the dangers of private fostering arrangements were highlighted in February 2000 when Victoria Climbié died after experiencing extreme abuse within such an arrangement. The subsequent Laming Report (2003) on her death detailed how there had been several occasions when practitioners might have intervened. While fostering of children is widespread as a form of child care across the globe, trafficked young people may be kept hidden within such arrangements. In 2010, the British Association for Adoption and Fostering launched a national campaign – Someone Else's Child – to raise awareness about such private fostering arrangements.

Neither Binta's 'aunt' nor her 'father' were relatives, although their accounts were, initially at least, considered more credible than her own. Her 'aunt' was the person she feared the most and it took fabricating illness for her to obtain the protection she needed. The language of family was used throughout, with 'aunts', 'uncles' and 'cousins' being benevolent terms for what were, in the cases we examined, exploitative and/or abusive relationships. Another young person was found to have been coerced into migrating to the UK under a similar guise: 'The young person was put on a plane by a man known to her as "Snakehead". She refers to him as being her uncle' (Interview 5).

'Uncle' has various meanings and interpretations and can indicate any elder male in many cultures around the world. The ways in which children are raised and socialised differ enormously across the globe and many households have a more complex family structure than the dominant Western model of the nuclear family which, as Mann (2001) argues, pervades the literature on child protection. Child protection is immersed in this understanding, with responses to trafficking falling into this paradigm (Bovarnick 2010). Exploiters may abuse the prevailing understanding of the 'nuclear' and 'extended' family struture that underpins Western assumptions about families. Indeed, children may have different roles in the family, acting as 'aunts' and 'uncles' themselves with varying levels of responsibilty, particularly during displacement and in situations of rapid social change. Again, this is an issue that somewhat separates younger children from older adolescents, and the latter may be assumed to be carrying familial and community responsibilites. If trafficking discourses are limited to assumptions about the trafficking of children, the different exploitative dynamics experienced by older young people may be lost from view or assumed to be normal and acceptable.

For example, differences in household composition, family and community structures were commented on by one practitioner who noted how assumptions about 'cultural' norms may hide abuse:

> I mean if you think about it, if you lived in Africa, if you lived in Cape Town, the societal norm is to have a house girl, yeah? She might be 13 or 14 but she will do the housekeeping, the cleaning and such like. So if you then go to live in England, your norm is to have a house girl. So, culturally, I think there's a . . . I think people are a bit scant sometimes, 'well, that's normal', if you're from that cultural background.
>
> (Interview 29)

Whilst calling elders 'aunt' or 'uncle' in certain countries of origin is common, more experienced practitioners noted the need to be cautious about uncritical assumptions that private foster care arrangements were acceptable, or that older young people might necessarily assume and accept specific roles within the home. Binta's case and others show the complexities involved when trying to ensure child protection while respecting diversity without colluding with prejudice and abuse. As Asmussen (2010) has outlined, child abuse occurs across all cultures and countries. Surveys suggest that at least 16 per cent of the population within Western cultures will experience some serious form of maltreatment during their childhood (ibid.).

'Culture' alone is not therefore an explanation for abuse, and nor is it easily defined. Citing the Victoria Climbié case, Philips (2007) argues that it is the impact 'culture' or 'race' can have on professional practice that makes minority ethnic children particularly vulnerable to abuse. Hence, there are dangers that need to be avoided when assessing particular nationalities or communities: 'On the one hand, a *pathologising* approach to black families may lead to unnecessarily coercive intervention and, on the other hand, a *cultural relativist* approach may lead to non-intervention when services are required' (Bernard and Gupta 2006). Such perceptions that either pathologise (regard minority ethnic people and their cultures as inherently problematic and in need of correction) or adhere to cultural relativism (maintain that all cultures are equally valid and that no one culture can criticise another) require ongoing awareness.

Associated with this is the need to question expectations that children and young people may assume particular roles within particular communities at different stages of their lifespan development.

Minority ethnic families may be both more and less likely to be subjected to child protection investigations due directly to the perceptions of professionals. Owen and Statham (2009) found that children from black and mixed ethnic backgrounds are overrepresented among children in the 'looked after' population, whereas Asian children tend to be underrepresented. They also suggested that there was greater unwillingness in some cultures to report concerns about a child's safety and greater uncertainty among professionals about how to respond appropriately. Between the two extremes of pathologising and cultural relativism, Korbin (2007) has outlined how the 'cultural competence' of professionals is key, in that it provides a useful balance and mid-point between these two extremes during assessments. Training in this model may be a helpful step forward for practitioners working in this area.

Our research noted that practitioners already had skills that, with knowledge and training in understanding these extremes of pathologising/relativism, were transferrable to different contexts. Trafficking often entails extreme forms of physical, emotional or sexual abuse and neglect, and a practitioner's knowledge of forms of abuse and their physical and behavioural signs can be utilised. Assumptions arising from informal profiling of communities, or about benevolence within 'communities', may each result in making cases invisible to child protection agencies.

A dominant awareness of trafficking for sexual exploitation

Children and young people are trafficked for a variety of reasons. As outlined in chapters 1 and 2, a 'sexual trafficking discourse' has emerged as the dominant story of trafficking within the UK, and arguably the rest of Europe (Jobe 2008). This 'story' has meant that some adult females have accessed help and services on this basis (Jobe 2010). While other forms of trafficking such as labour exploitation, domestic servitude and forced marriage are now beginning to emerge on the policy agenda, there is a danger that trafficking for sexual exploitation may override these and other more hidden forms of trafficking. That is, the process of trafficking may be assumed to be all about sexual exploitation rather than a range of different forms of exploitation.

Data generated in this study reflected the more dominant forms, with sexual exploitation being referred to 220 times, domestic servitude 40 times and benefit fraud 26 times. Agricultural labour, begging or pickpocketing, credit card fraud, drug-related trafficking, forced marriage, intercountry adoption, restaurant work, work in nail bars, trafficking for the purposes of surrogacy and other forms of bonded labour generated fewer than ten references each. Practitioners who had worked with cases of sexual exploitation of indigenous children within the UK were better attuned to indicators of sexual exploitation than to the indicators of other forms of exploitation. Throughout the research, where there had originally been a focus on trafficking for the purpose of sexual exploitation, it was increasingly recognised that the trafficking process often involved a range of different forms of exploitation and abuse: 'It would be children who are brought in for domestic purposes, children who were brought in for adoption, or children who were brought here for prostitution' (Interview 009).

With the advent of the Sexual Offences Act 2003, trafficking into, within and out of the UK for the purposes of sexual exploitation was made illegal under sections 57 to 59. Trafficking for other purposes came under the Asylum and Immigration (Treatment of Claimants, etc.) Act 2004. The potential for prosecution to occur as a result of other forms of trafficking has grown. This has also meant that the trafficking of boys or young men could begin to be better understood:

> Now we deal with domestic servitude and benefit fraud, rather than sexual exploitation. So we do get a better balance. We deal with sexual exploitation but we find the volume of child trafficking that we are uncovering is domestic servitude and benefit fraud. So, therefore, you are going to get a better balance of gender.
>
> (Interview 2)

The trafficking of boys and young men: understanding the impact of gender

As noted in chapters 1 and 2, practitioners may consciously or unconsciously rely on images that are prevalent in media portrayals of trafficking. Perhaps reflecting the high media exposure that trafficking for the purpose of sexual exploitation receives, our research found practitioners predominantly focusing on trafficking for sexual exploitation. While diverting attention away from other forms of exploitation, the preoccupation with trafficking for the purpose of sexual exploitation also entails a gender bias as girls are commonly perceived as more vulnerable to sexual exploitation than boys. This may be partly because practitioners still tend to work with a majority of girls within sexual exploitation services. As one practitioner explained:

> We have about 50 new referrals a year and most of them are young women. We did try to address that by launching some materials, you

know posters and contact cards aimed specifically at boys. That has had a little bit of success in that we've had about 6 boys out of 50 young people this year.

(Interview 27)

The preoccupation with sexually exploited girls and young women makes this particular group more visible. With growing public awareness, practitioners may develop a heightened sensitivity around this issue and may specifically look out for cases of sexually exploited girls. While this enhanced awareness is welcomed, and long overdue, it is still limited and concentrated in particular localities where campaign work and project development have taken place, or where proximity to an airport has generated concern. Consequently, understanding is still limited and practitioners may be more likely to identify and define girls as 'trafficked' than boys. This happens in the face of growing evidence of boys being trafficked for the purpose of sexual exploitation. One practitioner noted: 'I think if we were concentrating on sexual exploitation we would recognise that boys are just as vulnerable for that, particularly Chinese boys' (Interview 10).

Many practitioners commented on how boys and young men were vulnerable to being trafficked for sexual exploitation as well as girls and young women. In 2006, 70 per cent of all unaccompanied or separated children in care were boys (Home Office 2008a: table 2k). That trafficking of children and young people concentrates on girls and young women can be seen as a reflection of gendered assumptions inherent within the discourse. This was something recognised in relation to sexual exploitation:

I think people do tend to focus on girls for the simple fact that people know more about girls. But I don't think that it . . . obviously, it doesn't exclude boys at all and I think it means that people really have to try harder to try and sort of look at the exploitation of boys.

(Interview 10)

The case study of Thomas explores this.

Case study: Thomas's story

Thomas, a 16-year-old British boy, had a history of neglect and had been abused by his uncle and cousin. His mother was unable to care for him and he had moved between different extended family placements, foster placements and several children's homes. Thomas was friendly with older men and there was a suspicion that he was given money for sex. He was also known to experience problems with alcohol and cannabis use. Questions were raised with regard to periods when he went missing. On return from being missing he often had large amounts of cash, several mobile phones and expensive items in his possession. When questioned, he did not want to talk about what was happening or where he was going.

On more than one occasion, overseas travel was arranged for Thomas, with him often going missing for periods of between two and six weeks. Alongside concerns over sexual exploitation, there were suspicions that he might have been involved with drug traffickers. Thomas's journeys were often staggered. For example, he went to one country and received instructions and tickets for travel to another country. Practitioners repeatedly tried to investigate how Thomas obtained the money and tickets for these trips but the circumstances remained unclear.

The sexual exploitation unit ultimately became involved and took his passport to prevent him from leaving the country again. Thomas did not see himself as being trafficked or at risk. When this was discussed with him, he asked, 'Why is the social worker worried about me now when they didn't care that my uncle abused me?'

Cases such as this demonstrate that trafficking of children and young people born in the UK can occur, involving movement within and out of the UK. The process of extended movement is complex and incorporates different forms of abuse and exploitation. The case illustrates that boys and young men are vulnerable to sexual exploitation and other forms of trafficking (see Lillywhite and Skidmore 2006 for further debate on this).

It was apparent from the case file notes that discussions with Thomas were always difficult, demonstrating the problems practitioners encounter when they are developing child-centred practice. In this case, the young person and the practitioner held different perceptions of the extent and nature of abuse and potential exploitation. Questions around Thomas's movements, potentially connected to trafficking out of the UK, were understandably considered by him to be less important than the abuse he had previously experienced from his uncle and the interventions to end his movement, which made him angry. This case illustrates some of the complex negotiations that need to take place with the young person. As discussed in chapter 2, these may be specific to work with adolescents, whom practitioners are committed to safeguarding while supporting them to make autonomous decisions about their transition to adulthood. The fact that practitioners felt it necessary to take Thomas's passport away from him might be seen as an infringement on a young person's rights, but it was necessary to secure his continued safety. These decisions cannot be taken lightly and practitioners need support and supervision to help them process casework in these complex circumstances.

Another example of how the sexual exploitation of boys appears to challenge existing gender stereotypes is illustrated by the following practitioner's account:

> I was at a tube station and there was a man there that looked to be in his fifties and a boy who looked to be mid to late teens and they weren't standing together . . . I knew something was wrong and I saw it, walked out and I thought 'this isn't right' and I walked back just to have another look, at which point the guy approached me and said 'oh he's just a little bit upset, his parents have had to go home sooner than he thought they would.' Because he looked respectable, because he came up and approached me and seemed quite happy to speak to me I took it at face value . . . I have a horrible feeling that I had bumped into someone at the moment he'd been handed over. And I'm afraid a teenage boy who looks as though he's got a strop on isn't necessarily someone you're going to rush to try and speak to at the time, and I regret not doing so.
>
> (Interview 15)

While the practitioner recalling this event had a 'gut feeling' that something was wrong, he did not act on his intuition. Perhaps his understanding of trafficking was informed by an underlying set of gendered assumptions, which in turn made it difficult for him to recognise a boy as sexually exploited.

There is a developing awareness of the needs of boys and young men and how interventions can be created to work sensitively with them (with a young men's forum created to work with them in this way – see the website of the National Working Group for Sexually Exploited Children and Young People). However, most services for sexually exploited children and young people tend to work with girls and young women.

If examining the process of trafficking is limited to a gendered perspective that works to a strict division between female 'victim' and male 'perpetrator', the complexities of the impact of abuse on both genders will be missed. Assumptions will prevail so that young men's experience of sexual exploitation will be overlooked. This is particularly pertinent, too, when addressing the gendered impact of poverty and war, which often channel boys and young men towards criminality or 'child soldiering' and girls and women towards enforced domestic servitude and sexual exploitation. The fact that boys may be sexually abused while working as child soldiers may be overlooked. Addressing the 'process of trafficking' means ensuring that the process is 'gender proofed', that is, assumptions about expected behaviours of young women and young men are challenged and addressed so that the full range of individual and specific needs are recognised.

The process of movement: 'internal' and 'international' trafficking

As noted above, the process of trafficking can include movement into, within and out of a specific country. It is rarely confined to one journey with a clear beginning and end to exploitation. Some practitioners preferred to maintain a focus on trafficking of British children within the UK, while others focused attention on children brought into the UK and then moved within and, potentially, out of the country. Practitioners' understanding of these different processes tended to be influenced by where their work was located. Practitioners located near airports experienced a wider range of cases of children being internationally trafficked, and therefore tended to hold a broader range of views about trafficking. These practitioners had a higher number of separated children and young people arriving from overseas who came to their attention and were more aware of the different forms of trafficking. To some extent, they rejected the concept of 'internal' trafficking: 'No, I think nobody would ever talk about indigenous kids as having been trafficked' (Interview 5).

Practitioners located further away from ports into the UK tended to refer to indigenous young people who were trafficked for sexual exploitation. Their focus was more directed towards work with young people who had lived in their area for a substantial time; the kinds of young people they had gained more experience in identifying; and for whom service delivery had already been developed. They understood trafficking as any movement, even for very short distances:

> when she gets into a car she is immediately trafficked. It's the movement and the travel that defines trafficking . . . because if you look at the definition there are three things, it's the means, it's the end and it's the act. So the act of transportation or moving them from one place to another place is happening. The end, the objective of doing all these things to these kids is to sexually exploit them. Because they haven't come from overseas . . . doesn't mean they're not trafficked because there is exploitation and there is transportation by means of coercion, grooming, all these things that were mentioned in the Palermo Protocol.
>
> (Interview 24)

This same practitioner went on to suggest: 'People think that trafficking has got to be foreign nationals coming across international borders. They don't realise about internal trafficking, they don't realise it could be UK nationals. There's still massive knowledge gaps' (Interview 24).

There are certainly differences between 'internal' and 'international' cases. Children from overseas will have additional barriers to overcome in relation to being heard, such as language ability and knowledge of services and systems within the UK. The lack of 'ontological security' (Hynes 2007; Chase *et al.*2008) inherent in their presence in the country, the effect of any lack of documentation and fear of ultimate deportation cannot be stressed enough. The lack of a person with 'parental responsibility' for them is another key area of difference – in the main, UK young people will have had this in their history, either through their own parents or through a local authority carrying parental responsibility. Young people from overseas may not have received such support. Separated young people may well have parents in their countries of origin. It is the deficit of a parent or advocate within the country that makes their experiences distinct from UK young people. This is explored further in chapter 7.

Conclusions

In conceptualising the entire process of trafficking it is important to remember that identification of a child as 'trafficked' may take months, if not years, to occur. Disclosure of abuse – and in the case of trafficking, coercion and deception – invariably takes time. When the jigsaw pieces of a young person's life are placed together by a practitioner during assessment, greater emphasis on the potential process of trafficking over time may allow for the individual young person's history and circumstances to be better understood and their unique needs and aspirations to be addressed. Identification needs to acknowledge the complex relationship between internal and international trafficking of young people, and needs to be sensitive to the impact of gendered expectations that influence young people's and adults' behaviours, and the interpretation of these behaviours. In addition, caution must be taken to prevent us from 'profiling' or 'othering' both victims and perpetrators, assuming, for example, that perpetrators are necessarily always from 'outside' the mainstream. This carries the danger of averting the gaze from other potential dynamics and realities.

The need to understand the entire process of trafficking will involve a practitioner in working over a sustained period of time with the young person, exploring through child-centred initiatives the young person's individual history, how they arrived and how they survive in the country. As noted, 'vulnerability' does not end once a young person arrives in the UK. Good practice developed through consultations with the NSPCC Child trafficking Advice and Information Line suggests that the National Referral Mechanism needs also to allow for identification to occur at different stages of this process (CEOP *et al.* 2011). A referral mechanism dominated by immigration and police-led agencies may miss the vulnerabilities of young people that can only be identified after sustained intervention and support.

Finally, the trafficking of young people into, within and out of the UK is a child protection issue that can be at the centre of analysis of global economic, political and societal changes. As such, the causes and consequences of the trafficking of young people are best understood as human rights abuses and child protection issues across the globe. The UNCRC provides the central premise for this understanding. While this is welcomed, we have noted caution in assuming children to be a homogeneous group, and noted the need for the specific dynamics of engaging with and supporting adolescents to be recognised.

The next chapter will explore further how trafficked young people are controlled and manipulated by their traffickers through coercion, violence and other mechanisms, including 'debts' owed and exploitation of children's lack of language skills. Such increased understanding of both the process and mechanism of control and the journeys undertaken by those who are trafficked can only improve interventions to prevent abuse and prosecute offenders.

5   The wall of silence

In the previous chapter, the length of time that it may take for a young person to be identified as trafficked was explored. In this chapter, this is investigated further by discussing another key finding from our research: that trafficking is often hidden behind a 'wall of silence'. This metaphor is used to describe the hidden nature of trafficking of young people and the environment of disbelief, denial and silence that surrounds it.

Practitioners interviewed in the study reported that the trafficking of young people was usually hidden and difficult to detect. This finding was echoed by the case files of trafficked children that were analysed for the study. Some case files depicted young people's stories in great detail and revealed how they were identified as trafficked, how they disclosed what had happened to them, or why they often remained silent. At other times, young people's case files were fragmented and difficult to make sense of. All case files, however, consistently revealed two overriding themes: first, that young people are frequently subjected to a plethora of pressures, which deter them from speaking out; and secondly, that practitioners do not always pick up on children's disclosures and frequently miss indicators of potential trafficking cases. These two themes constitute the two sides of the wall of silence. They can be seen as mutually reinforcing, perpetuating the silence surrounding the trafficking of young people.

The wall of silence plays an instrumental role in stifling concerns about trafficked young people. It furthermore serves to protect those who traffic, abuse and exploit young people by keeping this crime hidden and by deterring its victims from speaking out. This chapter examines both sides of the wall and elaborates on some of the underlying reasons that allow the wall of silence to persist. It will argue that there is a need to be attentive to the realities of trafficking of young people in our immediate environment, to acquire skills to better identify potential cases of trafficking, and to better support child victims and survivors.

One side of the wall: young people find it difficult to speak

Reasons why young people find it difficult to speak out about their experiences of being trafficked are complex and diverse. They relate, among other factors, to young people's sense of agency, their particular vulnerabilities, and to fear and various forms of control and coercion employed by traffickers to intimidate and deter trafficked young people from seeking help. These are elaborated below.

Young people's agency

Young people's sense of agency in the trafficking process has traditionally evoked much debate. The debate centres on issues of 'consent' and 'victimology' and relies heavily on constructed distinctions between 'adults' and 'children' and the associated rights, responsibilities and competencies (Breuil 2008: 226–7). As explained in chapters 1 and 2, theoretical distinctions between 'adults' and 'children' may gloss over important differences with regard to individual characteristics, including a person's age, maturity, gender, capabilities and vulnerabilities, as well as protective factors and resilience. In essence, they can tend to assume homogeneity as opposed to recognising differences within lifespan development. These factors frequently shape young people's sense of agency and inform how they understand and contextualise their experiences of being trafficked. Young people's experiences of trafficking are inevitably varied and inherently personal.

As Bovarnick has argued, the Palermo Protocol constitutes children as victims per se and nullifies a young person's consent regardless of their own sense of agency. It classifies child trafficking as a crime, thereby placing trafficked young people under the age of 18 firmly in a safeguarding arena (Bovarnick 2010). While the Palermo Protocol renders a child's consent to being trafficked invalid, issues around consent are often complex in practice. Breuil (2008) argues that the legal definition only allows for children to assume the passive role of 'victim', which challenges observations recounted by the practitioners Breuil interviewed who were working with trafficked young people in Marseille. These social and youth workers reported varying degrees of powerlessness and control felt by young people under 18 over their trafficking situations (2008: 227). In some cases, young people are able to influence the outcome of their trafficking experiences to a certain degree, which may reinforce their sense of agency. This, however, does not diminish our safeguarding responsibilities towards trafficked young people. It is maintaining this balance, protecting on the one hand while supporting the development of self-determination on the other (as was illustrated by Thomas's case in chapter 4), which is the specific challenge to practitioners.

Young people may not see themselves as 'trafficking victims'

Our research revealed that some trafficked young people do not see themselves as abused or exploited, let alone 'trafficked'. This can reinforce
their silence and undermine their ability to understand their experiences in
relation to exploitation. Young people's self-definition, or frequently lack
thereof, as 'trafficking victims' needs to be understood in the context of the
existing heterogeneity with regard to what it means to be a 'young person'.

Young people's experiences of being trafficked are shaped by their individual journeys, their relationship with their traffickers and the geo-politi-
cal, cultural, religious, socio-economic and gendered narratives in which
they have grown up, as well as the personal circumstances in their home,
community or country of origin. As noted, concepts like 'childhood' and
'home' are normative and socially constructed (Breuil 2008). They carry
different meanings, particularly for migrant young people. While, for
many, the concept of 'home', for instance, generally conjures up images of
'warmth', 'belonging' or 'safety', such a notion may not exist in many parts
of countries from which migrant or trafficked young people originate. This
is not to imply that all internationally trafficked young people come from
war-torn countries or abusive families, or to insinuate that all British young
people have loving and prosperous homes. As already noted in chapter 4, it
is, however, useful to be mindful of inherently Westernised, normative con-
notations that we may associate with our conceptualisation of 'home' when
we examine the stories of migrant and trafficked children who often do not
have a safe home to return to.

Similar considerations apply to the concept of 'childhood', which may
entail different cultural notions around what constitutes 'exploitation' and
'acceptable treatment' of young people. As the previous chapter discussed,
internationally trafficked young people frequently come from environments
in which certain forms of child labour are considered acceptable and indeed
necessary for survival. Trafficked young people may have internalised such
norms and may be informed by notions of 'childhood' that are vastly different from standards prevailing in the UK. One practitioner explained: 'Some
of the Chinese boys who are over 15 would think that "why shouldn't I be
working? I have come here to get a better life and, yes, money has exchanged
hands for me but I know it's illegal but what is the problem?"' (Interview
10). Another practitioner recounted a case of a girl who was trafficked for
the purpose of marriage: 'She said at the time she did not mind this as she
thought it would be better than living a miserable life in Africa' (CS001).

In this way, trafficked young people have often internalised notions of
what is acceptable treatment of children that are rooted in the context of
their countries of origin. As one practitioner noted:

They have a different understanding of whether that's right or not based on why they would want to leave the country they're coming from . . . just like domestic servitude and just like illegal working or working in various restaurants – to them that might be something of value and they don't see themselves as being exploited or abused. So there very much can be a discrepancy between what they think is okay in terms of how they're treated and what really is okay, from our standards and from our perspective.

(Interview 29)

This shows that child protection standards vary considerably across the world. In war-torn countries, where human rights abuses are prolific, young people may have experienced or witnessed extreme forms of violence from an early age and may have come to accept these as a 'normal' part of life. This is not to imply, however, that such experiences do not have a detrimental effect on children who grow up in environments in which they are exposed to high levels of violence. It is merely suggested here that prolonged exposure to such adversities may lead to young people to 'expect' abusive treatment and exploitation. Furthermore, such experiences may prevent young people from identifying themselves as 'victims' of abuse or exploitation and are likely to curb children's efforts to disclose what has happened and seek help.

Practitioners reported that, at some point, usually after entering the care system, trafficked young people may realise that their experiences of trafficking are outside the 'normal/acceptable' realm and begin to understand what they have gone through in the context of exploitation:

Because once the experience changes, like either come into the asylum system . . . they transfer from the care of a person who suspectedly trafficked them to the care of Social Services, and they're having access to education, health services and socialising . . . they are then able to compare their life beforehand and their life now, and then they can identify that themselves that they have been maltreated. Have I ever heard a young person use the word 'trafficked'? No.

(Interview 9)

Understanding young people's vulnerabilities

Human trafficking, as well as migration in general, has frequently been explained through the concept of 'push' and 'pull' factors. However, as noted in the previous chapter, human trafficking is a complex process rather than a 'one-off event'. It is more useful to think in terms of young people's 'vulnerabilities' rather than 'push/pull factors' when exploring underlying causes of trafficking, whether these are individual vulnerabilities or those constructed through immigration regimes. The research revealed that many trafficked young people had experiences of significant loss in their lives; many were orphaned and had been looked after by a series of different people in the extended family or community until they were left to their own devices, often homeless and destitute while still relatively young: 'She had no one to look after her and the neighbour was fed up of looking after her' (CS006).

Typically, a series of adverse events had made young people vulnerable to abuse or exploitation prior to being trafficked. In some cases, abuse in the country of origin had initiated the trafficking process or had motivated the young person to try to escape an adverse situation in search of a better life abroad, as the composite case study of Wen Xi illustrates.

Case study: Wen Xi's story

Wen Xi was a toddler when her mother died. After her mother's death, her father suffered from depression and could not cope. He died when she was six. Wen Xi lived in a small village where the abuse of human rights was routine and where there were few, if any, jobs. Many people lived in poverty. Wen Xi was then taken in by an elderly neighbour whom she referred to as 'grandmother'. Her 'grandmother' looked after her and sent her to school. When Wen Xi was ten, her 'grandmother' passed away and left her in the care of a couple who lived in the same community. After Wen Xi started living with the couple, they started abusing and exploiting her. The couple made her work long hours in a physically demanding and potentially dangerous job. Wen Xi was also sexually abused by the man and accused by his wife of having an affair with him. The wife subsequently maltreated Wen Xi physically and emotionally.

When Wen Xi was 14, she was approached by a man in her village who told her that he was aware of her difficulties and offered to help her get out of the country. After the couple tried to force Wen Xi to work as a prostitute, she decided to take the man up on his offer. The man told Wen Xi he would arrange her journey to leave China in order to escape to a safe place. Wen Xi was subsequently trafficked to the UK for the purpose of domestic servitude and sexual exploitation. After a period of being entrapped within a family home, where she undertook childcare and unpaid domestic work, a friend of the family raped her. She was then placed in a brothel from which she managed to escape.

While young people with a history of domestic violence, abandonment or lack of consistent care are forced to look after themselves from a relatively young age, they often remain vulnerable to abuse and exploitation, including trafficking. With no designated adult carer to assume responsibility for their protection and well-being, young people may have become accustomed to fending for themselves. As a result, they may appear mature yet may not have received the parenting or guidance to develop the skills necessary to make good judgements, to assess risks adequately and to make safe choices.

All of these factors may contribute to the way young people understand their role in the trafficking process. Despite putting themselves at risk of abuse and exploitation, young people may feel that they are exerting control over their lives by taking active steps to escape an adverse situation. This perceived sense of agency, however, may also lead them to 'blame themselves' for what has happened, which may act as a deterrent from disclosing the abuse and seeking help. This contributes to the maintenance of the wall of silence.

Young people may be too afraid to disclose

Young people's vulnerabilities are often specifically targeted and exploited by traffickers. Practitioners mention that even though each trafficked young person carries their own particular set of vulnerabilities and has a unique story to tell, some 'patterns' feature repeatedly in trafficking cases.

One reoccurring theme was that traffickers are highly skilled in manipulating or coercing young people into staying silent. Control mechanisms often represent a continuum of overt and covert forms and range from subtle to extremely violent forms of coercion and control. Traffickers may, for instance, intimidate a young person by threatening to hurt them, their friend or a family member. In many cases, threats will be followed up by actual violence and abuse towards the trafficked young person or someone close to them. One practitioner in the study recalled: 'She talks about punching, kicking, pulling hair, throwing girls around naked and being burned with cigarettes' (CS019). In the face of such overt cruelty, young people may decide that it is safer for them to comply with their traffickers' demands rather than risk their lives by seeking help in an unknown and potentially hostile environment.

Traffickers may also tell young people that they owe money for the transit or travel documents and that they have to work it off. One practitioner mentioned the 'low rates of pay he was receiving for manual labour . . . he was repaying debt' (Interview 15). Furthermore, traffickers may threaten to report young people to the authorities in order to evoke fear of deportation. Young people who have been trafficked from abroad are particularly vulnerable to such forms of intimidation as they often have little or no command of English and tend to be unfamiliar with the UK child protection system. They may not be aware of their human rights or entitlements under UK law. In addition, they may carry a deep-rooted fear or mistrust of authorities and adults in general, which may stem from traumatic past experiences. As one practitioner mentioned: '[He] felt scared about his new surroundings' (CS025). Another practitioner explained: 'If people are raping you several times on a daily basis . . . you're not going to rush to speak to someone else and say what's wrong in case they do the same' (CS001).

Young people may find it hard to believe that there are professionals and agencies that are able and willing to help them. Traffickers can play on these notions and reinforce the young people's fear of authorities by making them believe that they have done something illegal and that it is in their own interest to remain hidden. As one practitioner argued: 'Knowing their rights in the UK doesn't necessarily change what's being held over them or what the deception is. That still appears to be stronger than what they think they're going to get from their rights in the UK' (Interview 13).

In addition, the research showed that traffickers manipulate young people into believing that they are not being abused or exploited. In some cases, grooming processes contributed to young people forming an attachment to their traffickers. Such identification with traffickers may distort the way young people interpret their experiences and prevent them from seeing themselves as exploited: 'Some Chinese girls that we knew had disappeared and had a "boyfriend". These girls didn't see themselves as exploited. They thought that this guy loved them' (Interview 11).

Young people may also experience a specific form of attachment to their traffickers that is sometimes referred to as 'Stockholm syndrome', a paradoxical psychological phenomenon whereby hostages feel empathy towards their captors. Although such feelings are irrational in the light of the danger or risk faced by the hostage, victims may interpret a lack of abuse from their captors as kindness or justify abuse by believing that traffickers are in fact protecting them. Again, these dynamics all contribute to the young person remaining quiet about the abuse, maintaining the wall of silence.

Young people may employ silence as a coping strategy

In addition to all the pressures noted above, young people may not speak out about the abuse that is happening because they have developed various coping mechanisms, including 'shutting off' emotionally or compartmentalising the pain attached to past traumatic experiences. As a result, some young people may simply not be ready to talk. They may remain silent in order to cope with what has happened to them, fearing that to start to uncover the abuse will be to open themselves to feelings that they cannot manage and that may undermine the coping mechanisms they have developed. In other words, maintaining silence is a way of maintaining control over their own mental health. This is not always adequately understood by practitioners. One practitioner noted: 'The young person was very skilled at deflecting people from finding out more about her, her past or the people with whom she associates. She is closed off emotionally and will not discuss her own safety' (CS025). In relation to a young male recently identified as trafficked, another practitioner recalled: 'he's got really high emotional needs, not used to disclosing anything' (Interview 26). Practitioners, particularly those who have a limited understanding of the impact of trafficking on young people, may find engaging with this group of young people frustrating. As one practitioner recalled: 'even with the very best social workers this child was extremely reluctant to disclose' (CS025).

Chase *et al.* (2008) have conducted research into the mental health and well-being of separated asylum-seeking children, providing a valuable insight into this area. Their study revealed that separated children had often experienced extreme trauma and loss in their countries of origin as well as during their journeys to the UK. As a result, many of the children in the study displayed a wide spectrum of emotional difficulties, ranging from anxiety, feelings of isolation and loss, disturbed sleep patterns, depression, headaches and eating disorders to more severe mental health issues requiring specialist help and in some cases hospitalisation. The research further found that young men were less likely to talk about their experiences and to seek help than young women. In addition, it was noted that mental health was conceptualised differently in the UK than in other countries from which many separated children originated. Some of these differences in understanding related to language, while others were linked to stigmatisation of mental health issues or different conceptualisations of specific emotional or psychological problems. There is a training need for practitioners to better understand these differences in order to successfully engage with separated and trafficked young people to break through the wall of silence and to enable young people to begin to disclose information about the abuse they have experienced.

We have noted above how, for a range of reasons, young people may remain silent about the abuse that has taken place. They may be misled into believing that their situation is 'normal', that they are to blame, or that if they were to report abuse, their future could be worse. Alternatively, they may be afraid that if they begin to speak about the abuse they have experienced, their own coping mechanisms may fall apart and they would collapse altogether. If practitioners assume that the young person is able to manage their own disclosure, they are colluding with the exploitation. However, as is noted throughout this book, the challenge for practitioners working with trafficked young people is in helping them to recognise the impact of the abuse while maintaining some sense of control over their own future development. In chapter 7 we explore some of the ways that a 'relationship based' approach to intervention can enable this process to occur. For now it is important to recognise how young people themselves can maintain the wall of silence. In addition, the wall is supported by practitioners who may find it difficult to recognise or acknowledge the abuse experienced by the young person. It is to this that we now turn.

On the other side of the wall: practitioners find it difficult to hear and believe young people's accounts

Our research revealed that practitioners experienced difficulties in hearing and believing young people's disclosures, which undermined identification of trafficking cases. Reasons for this are complex and, among other factors, relate to the challenging environment of social work, practitioners' varying degrees of knowledge and expertise in the field of trafficking of young people, and a culture of disbelief that permeates the practice of professions coming into contact with trafficked young people.

Silence because of limited resources and competing priorities

There is a significant body of evidence showing that very young infants (particularly those under one) are at the greatest risk of significant harm and death (Cawson *et al.* 2000). Recently, the tragic and well-publicised case of baby Peter Connelly's death has once more highlighted this group of children as particularly vulnerable. While this might explain why the current UK child protection system is particularly geared towards safeguarding infants and young children, there is, as we have argued, significant concern that the system may be less effective in meeting the safeguarding needs of older children and teenagers who frequently tend to come to the attention of children's services as 'children in need' rather than 'child protection' cases (Rees *et al.*2010; Pearce 2009). As noted, this also affects trafficked young people since the majority of known cases tend to involve older children and teenagers (CEOP 2009).

Social work tends to take place in a pressurised environment and is characterised by limited resources. As a result, social workers tend to face a heavy and varied workload, having constantly to deal with competing priorities. Because infants are particularly vulnerable, this may mean that social workers prioritise this group of children over older ones. Practitioners are often required to make judgement calls based on the information they have, which may be rather limited in trafficking cases. Although some young people may present with obvious indicators of exploitation and abuse, many may divulge only a small fraction of the whole story. If there are language barriers, this can delay investigations into potential trafficking cases even further. Social workers may feel that they are venturing into unfamiliar territory and may inadvertently turn their attention to cases which are 'easier' to define and respond to. The 'hot potato' effect may ensue, whereby trafficked children are passed around services (see chapter 6 for further discussion of this effect). This can be exacerbated further by the fact that many trafficked young people go 'missing' and continue to be at risk of being re-trafficked. Agencies may struggle to keep up with the whereabouts of a trafficked young person if the child drops off the radar.

Silence because of misunderstanding the trafficking process

Trafficking is a complex process and an area that may involve considerable ambiguity, with information about trafficking cases often patchy and inconsistent. This may make practitioners feel that they do not know enough about a case to identify a young person as trafficked. Our research has shown that it requires a high level of skill and knowledge to accurately interpret indicators of trafficking and to work with a young person over a period of time in order to develop the level of trust needed for a child to feel safe to disclose what has happened. Many local authorities have not yet developed an adequate knowledge base around trafficking and many practitioners may not have had access to any training in this area. As a result, trafficked young people may go unnoticed. Even if a trafficking case is suspected, practitioners may lack the relevant experience or resources to act on this information, which means that cases may get 'lost'. This means that the the trafficking of children and young people remains silenced, hidden from practitioners and the agencies they work with.

Our research also showed that there was a lack of country-specific information available in some local authorities. As noted in chapter 4, a limited knowledge of the circumstances under which children are trafficked undermines practitioners' ability to adequately interpret information that may relate to potential trafficking cases. One practitioner noted:

> I think that where it gets lost in a local authority is that because a trafficked child or a smuggled child or a child that is presented without any parents, they all get labelled under the umbrella of a Section 20 child. So there isn't anything really, or any person within a local authority that

is keeping abreast of the different experiences that children are coming into the local authority with.

(CS020)

As the previous chapter discussed, the research revealed a range of misconceptions regarding different ethnic communities, their cultural practices and normative systems, specifically relating to thresholds in terms of sexual and labour exploitation, and the value of human life in general. As Bovarnick (2010) and chapter 4 have shown, practitioners' views are not always based on firsthand experience of working with trafficking cases but are frequently informed by popular discourses, including media reports or hearsay. One practitioner, for example, described 'trafficking' as follows:

Bought – money changed hands. If you read the internet reporting, the media reporting, there are hospitals in Nigeria where girls go to have babies and they sell them. . . . And that's where I've read about these Nigerian hospitals where you can buy babies.

(Interview 15)

The practitioner continued:

I've not dealt with anything from Africa at all but I get the impression that with African girls from some states there's much more of a tradition of selling them off as slaves effectively and so that's when those sorts of considerations would apply here.

This lack of identification, and of recording of cases as trafficked, results in a continued silence within which trafficking is hidden from view.

Silence through misunderstood consent

In addition to not enough being known about trafficking and about specific countries of origin, the research revealed a plethora of misconceptions that created assumptions that young people come to the UK of their own free will. This misunderstanding of young people as actively consenting to the abuse they experienced was demonstrated through references to young people as being 'wilfully trafficked' or as 'accomplices' in the trafficking process (Bovarnick 2010). One practitioner argued: 'It must inevitably beg the question whether they were consenting or not . . . the fact that someone doesn't run off may lead people to be a bit more suspicious' (Interview 30).

As explained above, many internationally trafficked children have internalised different standards relating to child protection from those found in the UK, again demonstrating how more training on 'culturally competent' models of child protection may be of benefit (Korbin 2007). Practitioners may not be aware of how the Palermo Protocol constitutes the issue of a trafficked young person's 'consent'. This may perpetuate the false notion that young people can indeed consent to being trafficked and thus 'agree' to being exploited and abused.

Practitioners' uncertainty with regard to whether migrant young people are covered under UK child protection legislation can impede their willingness and ability to seriously investigate and identify cases of child trafficking, putting trafficked young people at further risk of abuse and exploitation. Pearce (forthcoming) explores different categories of consent as they are used in practice by child care professionals and by young people themselves in their everyday lives. This work, along with a continued focus on the need to better understand the safeguarding of neglected adolescents (Coleman 2011; Rees *et al.*2010), will advance ways of helping young people to manage the impact of the abuse they have undergone. These are needed to begin to break through the wall of silence described here. Our research revealed that practitioners' understanding of trafficking relied, to varying degrees, on preconceived notions about particular nationalities, forms of exploitation and oversimplified ideas of what a 'typical victim' might look like. Such notions were often linked to 'gender' and 'culture'. While the previous chapter discussed how these misconceptions relate to the trafficking process and children's vulnerabilities, this chapter picks up these themes by exploring how they contribute to the wall of silence. It is argued here that 'profiling' both traffickers and trafficking victims according to nationality, ethnicity, age or gender can facilitate this silence and hinder the identification of trafficking cases.

Silence perpetuated through lack of awareness of cultural and linguistic diversity

As the previous chapter highlighted, practitioners are not always sufficiently aware of the warning signs associated with trafficking, or they may at times be blinded by imagined or real cultural and linguistic diversities. Our research found a 'gap' in communication that frequently could only be overcome with the help of a highly skilled interpreter. For instance, cultural variations in using terms to describe family relations could present a challenge for practitioners and hinder identification. According to one practitioner:

> It is around understanding what the use of language is. So somebody, I will give a couple of simple examples of that – a young person might

call somebody 'uncle' and you would initially view that as a blood relative and quite often that is not the case.

(Interview 5)

The lack of clarity surrounding adults who accompany or appear to care for a migrant young person may mean that practitioners struggle to identify and investigate potential trafficking cases, particularly if it is difficult to establish the biological relationship or legal custodianship of the young person. Because concepts of family and community often do not translate literally into the UK context, this makes it difficult for practitioners to correctly interpret young people's accounts of their experiences and to appropriately identify risk factors.

The research highlighted language as a crucial link connecting communities, which at times kept young people isolated and prevented them from seeking help outside their communities.

She apparently meets two people at the airport who are speaking her language and then goes to stay with them for two weeks. We often get these so we know that this set-up isn't right. People who are strangers . . . People that look like them or speak their language or they overhear them, they approach them and these people automatically take them in. You get some of them staying with people for the duration of their claim, which could be months. It astounds us how many of these people will take in strangers! I guess you could think of it in a way of community support. But at the same time, if you're considering that some of these people have families, you'd tend to wonder if you would allow a complete stranger into your home when you have young children, when you don't know who they are. They could be a risk of any sort. So I think basically these people are people that they do know, or have had contact with, but don't wish us to know who they really are.

(Interview 23)

In the context of safeguarding young people, poorly informed notions about linguistic identities run the danger of oversimplifying the often complex composites of communities while reducing young people's identities to the language they speak. Such a limited understanding of language as a signifier of belonging to a specific group denies the importance of other factors, such as ethnicity, religion, class, age, gender, place of birth or abode, level of education, marital status and economic resources, and others that significantly shape a person's identity and experiences.

It was often assumed that a common language seemed to automatically tie young people to a community, which could act as a source of support.

However, at times this also made young people more vulnerable to being targeted by traffickers:

> And again, the people that are trafficking them know that they're most likely to trust someone who speaks their own language. So if they've come from being trafficked with an agent that's brought them in who's speaking their own language and says to them, 'this is going to happen, the people are speaking English to you are not the people you want to tell anything to'.
>
> (Interview 14)

Cultural and linguistic identification was also often seen as paramount for matching trafficked young people with foster placements. While same-ethnicity placements can offer a cultural link to a young person and facilitate communication, the research found that some placements with same-ethnicity foster parents or private fostering arrangements were not ideal and, in some cases, made a trafficked young person vulnerable to further exploitation or abuse. In essence, the chosen placement could further silence the young person while the environment within which they were living continued to abuse or failed to facilitate communication about previous experiences of exploitation. One practitioner argued against a same-culture placement as she had encountered resistance from the young person in her care: 'Because it could be quite organised. I mean it's only speculation but I have done a lot of thinking around it and wondering why would you so desperately not want to be with carers from your own racial background?' (Interview 28).

While there are many benefits in finding a culturally and ethnically appropriate placement for separated young people, we noted the need for practitioners to exercise caution in assuming that a migrant young person is always well cared for within his or her own community or extended family. The research shows that it is crucial to examine a young person's well-being in private fostering arrangements. If the placement is not able to facilitate disclosure of exploitation and enable the young person to open up about the impact of their previous experiences, it will contribute to the maintenance of the wall of silence, hiding details of young people's trafficking experiences.

Many practitioners in our research were able to pinpoint trends in the changing dynamics and models of trafficking as stories of trafficked young people from particular parts of the world kept repeating themselves. As patterns emerged, practitioners were able to contextualise the experiences of young people better, to identify trafficked children and young people more easily and to respond to their needs more adequately. As a result, this was a successful way of beginning to break through the wall of silence. One practitioner noted:

> There are a lot of Chinese young people going missing from [Care Home X] and there are suspicions that the traffickers are aware of [it]. There are also suspicions that there are people living at [Care Home X] that are involved in trafficking.
>
> (Interview 9)

Another practitioner argued:

> Notice how you have nail shops . . . depending on where you were, a large number of Korean, Chinese, these types of nationalities. The same thing applies for us, we see that definitely, particular nationalities end up in particular situations. Don't know what it is, don't know why, it just happens to be a trend.
>
> (Interview 12)

As noted in chapter 4, while 'profiling' seemed to help make sense of the complex nature of trafficking, it also formed generalised assumptions about particular nationalities or ethnic groups. The review of the 37 case studies undertaken for this research showed that each trafficking case was unique and deserved to be investigated and responded to with a tailored care plan and adequate service provision. That said, when practitioners were able to identify generic patterns within their work with trafficked young people, they were provided with evidence that they could use to argue for extra resources or for particular interventions. As has been noted through the work of NSPCC CTAIL, the collation of evidence of need provides a useful tool for fundraising and campaigning for resource allocation. While caution is needed to prevent simplistic profiling of cases, the collation of repeated patterns of forms of abuse can be useful in developing evidence for resources and challenging the wall of silence.

Silence through the culture of disbelief: stifling concern and impeding identification

The research revealed a 'culture of disbelief' which serves to stifle concerns about potentially trafficked children and impedes practitioners' ability to identify trafficking cases. This means that young people's stories were frequently heard but not understood. While the culture of disbelief ties in with the pressurised environment of practice, practitioners' training needs and the common misconceptions that we discussed previously, there are a number of additional factors, which contribute to this part of the wall of silence.

Practitioners may find children's stories relating to their experiences of trafficking difficult to make sense of. Disclosure in trafficking cases is rarely 'neat'. It rarely takes place in consecutive order. Rather, as discussed in chapter 4, disclosures tend to happen over time and can resemble a jig-saw puzzle that needs to be pieced together by a team of highly skilled professionals. More often than not, young people's accounts of their experiences may have gaps and be full of discrepancies. This may be because of language or cultural barriers that cause a 'gap' in communication. Or it may be that young people reveal their histories bit by bit, not necessarily in chronological order, but at a time and in a way that feels safe. Young people may omit parts of their stories because they may feel ashamed or be too traumatized to relive their experiences by retelling them. The psychological effects associated with post-traumatic stress disorder may further impede a young person's ability to accurately recall an event.

Some young people may purposely give a distorted or incomplete account of events because they may not trust a practitioner or be wary of the consequences a full disclosure might carry. As mentioned previously, young people may have been threatened and 'coached' by their traffickers to tell a particular story. For practitioners, this may imply hearing the same story over and over again, which may make a case appear fabricated. Some of the young people's disclosures may truthfully reflect their experiences but seem so horrific or far-fetched that practitioners may find them hard to believe. In these cases, professionals may resort to dismissing young people's stories as 'fiction' in order not to have to deal with such challenging information. Unless a practitioner has a sound understanding of the nature and dynamics of trafficking, these factors can breed mistrust and may undermine practi-tioners' willingness and ability to develop the skills and sensitivity needed to accurately interpret young people's accounts and to successfully identify trafficking cases. We explore this below, drawing on extracts from inter-views with practitioners to illustrate the points made.

Practitioners may see trafficking as an immigration rather than a child protection issue

In the past decade, UK policy debates around trafficking have been linked to the areas of immigration and child protection. While some practition-ers embrace a child-centred model of practice, our study found that other practitioners predominantly understand trafficking as an immigration issue. This 'immigration-centred discourse' tends to undermine practice with traf-ficked young people by promoting a sceptical view of trafficking victims (Bovarnick 2010). This discourse is frequently based on the assumption that young people may (falsely) claim to be trafficking victims in order to improve their chances of making successful asylum claims and to gain access to services. One practitioner argued: 'They come in, they claim to be children . . . they know if they claim to be children they will be put in a children's home rather than a detention centre' (CS011). Trafficked young people are, within this discourse, conceptualised as a drain on national resources rather than as maltreated young people who have safeguarding needs. For instance, a practitioner recounting a case of a young woman trafficked from Asia suggested: 'A cynic might say she was trying to get money out of social services. She was pregnant at the time' (Interview 12).

Our research revealed a tangible level of scepticism among some practitioners around the 'genuineness' of trafficking victims. This 'culture of disbelief' meant that young people's accounts might be dismissed rather than fully investigated, as the following practitioner recalled: 'This child has a very vivid imagination. I'm not even going to record a lot of our conversation because it's clearly not true' (CS011). In this instance, the young person concerned was found to have been trafficked and to have suffered considerable physical abuse both during the journey to the UK and within the country, carrying out domestic work.

Practitioners who conceptualise trafficking as an immigration issue frequently attribute a high level of agency to young people, implying that they plan to come to the UK and that they may consciously fabricate stories about being trafficked in order to exploit the system. The study found that such assumptions existed in different agencies that come into contact with trafficked young people and affected the way practitioners responded to them. One practitioner mentioned:

> I know that she's been in front of a jury and told a story about being raped over there. I know she wasn't believed. I know they wouldn't believe that the guy had been trafficking her . . . I mean we are asking the court to believe a 15-year-old girl against four or five adults.
>
> (Interview 13)

The culture of disbelief reflects many of the existing hierarchical power structures that are engrained in our society, privileging professionals over 'lay persons', adults over young people, UK nationals over migrants, and men over women. It creates an environment, in which practitioners tend to doubt and dismiss the accounts of trafficked young people. It is born out of a profound confusion relating to whether the trafficking of young people is an immigration or a child protection issue. In line with other chapters in this book, it is argued here that trafficking is a form of child abuse and, as such, should be seen first and foremost as a child protection issue and that young people trafficked from abroad have the same rights under UK child protection legislation as UK citizens. It is paramount that practitioners are made aware of this in order to better safeguard trafficked young people.

Conclusion

The wall of silence that surrounds trafficking is a major barrier to the successful identification of trafficked young people. Consisting of two sides, it silences young people's voices while preventing practitioners from seeing the realities of trafficking in the UK.

This chapter explored some of the reasons why the wall of silence exists and persists. On the one hand, young people find it difficult to speak out and find help. This may tie in with their own sense of agency and responsibility for their circumstances. For various reasons discussed in this chapter, some young people do not see themselves as trafficking victims. We have noted how many trafficked young people have experienced long and complex stories of abuse and exploitation, which may be difficult to recount or too traumatic to recall. These young people may still be under the control of their traffickers – even if they have left an acute situation of exploitation and abuse. They may be fearful and mistrustful of adults; they may not speak any English and have little knowledge of their new surroundings. If they do manage to overcome these obstacles, they may be met with scepticism and a culture of disbelief.

Practitioners, on the other hand, work in a pressurised and challenging environment, constantly having to juggle competing priorities and working within the constraints of limited resources. While our study highlighted pockets of good practice, it also showed some shortcomings in current practice. The wall of silence presents us with specific challenges that need to be addressed in order to better safeguard trafficked young people. This chapter revealed a number of training needs that should be addressed in order to enable practitioners to identify and work with trafficked young people more confidently. The trafficking of young people is a notoriously challenging area of work, filled with ambiguity and grey areas. Practitioners need to be equipped with extensive knowledge of the trafficking process, and of young people's vulnerabilities as well as their health, safety, educational and care needs. Specific cultural training relating to countries from which trafficked young people originate, as well as close collaboration with specialist interpreters, can help to reduce cultural and linguistic barriers and counteract common misconceptions. This would improve practitioners' abilities to contextualize young people's accounts and enable them to pick up on signs of potential trafficking cases more easily.

The wall of silence works as an established and effective mechanism to cover up and perpetuate the crime of the trafficking of young people. As such, it will take time and require effort to dismantle. There are many steps we can take to break down the wall from both sides. We can encourage trafficked young people to break the silence by creating a safe environment for them to speak out. We can also render UK practice more child-centred and work to dispel the culture of disbelief.

The conclusion drawn from this chapter lies in opening our eyes to the realities of the trafficking of young people in the UK. Based on the evidence presented here, we should give young people the benefit of the doubt, be willing to listen to their stories and become alert to the signs of trafficking, however incoherent or subtle they may be.

We move now to look more specifically at the different roles practitioners from different agencies can play in identifying and supporting trafficked young people, arguing first in chapter 6 that all agencies have a role, and then in chapter 7 that there are some specialist needs that require a particular agency response.

6 Universal services for trafficked young people

Previous chapters have explored the process of trafficking and the ways in which it is hidden from view. They have looked at how disclosure of the young person's account can rely on practitioners' understandings and scope to intervene and on the young person's willingness or capacity to disclose and work with service providers. This chapter draws on the research findings to argue that all professionals working in the range of universal children's services have a role to play in identifying and supporting trafficked young people. However, as noted by an interviewee, for this to function, staff from universal services need to be aware of safeguarding issues:

> the challenge that the government has given Safeguarding Children Boards is that the staff working in universal services and the third sector – the voluntary, private and faith sectors – they need to be people who have an awareness of safeguarding children . . . awareness of these issues [and] that the world is a complicated place . . .
>
> (Interview 19)

As we have argued, the 'trafficking' of young people under the age of 18 is a child protection/safeguarding issue, meaning that it is essential that practitioners from the full range of services are trained and equipped to identify and work with the young people concerned. By default, this means that a truly multi-agency approach to safeguarding requires practitioners from all services to be aware of and able to respond to the needs of trafficked young people.

To develop these points the chapter moves through five stages. First, it argues for agencies to understand when and why specific referral of the case on to a particular agency for intervention is appropriate, while simultaneously addressing the need for 'ownership' of casework so that the young person is not passed from 'pillar to post'. In this context it explores the 'hot potato' effect, where the young person is passed between services, each of whom resists ownership of the case. The reasons and mechanisms for this are discussed.

Secondly, it draws on examples from interventions led by health service practitioners to illustrate the important relationship between health (sexual, mental and physical health) and the well-being of trafficked young people.

Thirdly, it illustrates the important role of youth justice workers in identifying histories of trafficking in their client group. This leads to the bigger question of how to challenge the inappropriate criminalisation of young people who have been victims of trafficking.

Fourthly, it looks at examples from education providers to explore the importance of practitioners being able to listen to, and engage with, the young person once identification has occurred.

Finally, the chapter considers the role that universal service providers can play in gathering evidence that can be used as intelligence to take cases against a perpetrator to court. Just as many of the interventions with trafficked young people may be falsely assumed to be the sole prerogative of child protection services, so too the 'job' of gathering evidence to prosecute abusers may been seen as police business. While there are some interventions that only the police can make, multiagency work with other service providers is essential in securing evidence that can be used as intelligence to disrupt or prosecute abusers.

These stages culminate in the conclusion to this chapter which argues for all service providers to receive training and support to identify and work with trafficked young people. While the essential features of multi-agency work are examined further in chapter 8, this chapter argues for all agencies to feel responsible for both the protection of the victim and prosecution of the abuser, and in situations where the boundary between victim and perpetrator is less clear, to be sensitive to the pressures on young people that may underpin offending behaviours.

'Pillar to post': the hot potato effect

For multi-agency work to be effective, responsibilities need to be genuinely shared, rather than it being allowed that a young person is passed from one agency to another, neither taking ownership of intervention. This is particularly important in cases where there is an absence of a legal guardian or key worker advocate for a child. Practitioners from the full range of services need to be aware of local policies and procedures to be followed after identification of cases where trafficking may have occurred. If a fully multi-agency policy is to be achieved, agencies need to know both when and why they should be using their own resources to support the young person and when, why and where to refer the case on.

Guidelines to support these decision-making processes are clearly laid out in the DCSF guidance (2007), which clearly advises each Local Safeguarding Children Board to have a well-publicised procedure for how cases of trafficking should be worked with in each local area. In addition, the 'child trafficking toolkit' (London Safeguarding Children Board 2011), piloted in 2009 and used by some local authorities since, provides helpful advice to agencies about how and when to intervene and, in particular, how to facilitate effective multi-agency work to protect trafficked young people.

Findings from our research identified concern that these different sources of guidance may be poorly observed, often leaving a 'hot potato' effect, where agencies refer the case on because they feel ill-equipped to manage it themselves, either through lack of knowledge and experience or through an apparent or actual lack of resources. This can result in the young person being passed from 'pillar to post' without any one agency accepting responsibility for key work and casework management.

As noted elsewhere, this 'passing on' of cases has long been of concern to practitioners working with 'problem' young people (Ayer and Preston-Shoot 2010). If the practitioner is fearful that their intervention may not be appropriate or sufficient to meet the child's needs, and that this may then reflect badly in an audit or inspection of their work, they may choose to refer the case on to another agency. 'There is that huge emphasis on accountability . . . there is a culture among different agencies and teams where they don't necessarily want to own decisions and the child is treated like a hot potato' (Interview 28).

For those agencies required to demonstrate 'outcomes' from a six-month or one-year intervention, evidence of 'success' with the trafficked young person might be hard, if not impossible, to provide. For example, if the young person is finding it difficult to integrate into a school, or if they go missing from accommodation, this might be noted as a 'failure' on the part of the service provider. This can mean that an agency might be unwilling to take on a potentially 'difficult' young person. For example, a practitioner noted that 'there is a tendency to not acknowledge the problem . . . Because often they are scared that if they acknowledge, they ought to put a response in place and they don't have the resources' (CS010).

In addition, some interviews with practitioners noted that 'trafficking' and the extent of the damage it causes to a young person can frighten practitioners and be difficult to acknowledge. Indeed, as noted in chapter 3, we as researchers needed to ensure that we undertook regular reviews and had general 'debriefings' about the impact the work was having on us and our ability to sustain engagement with the issues involved. If there is no culture of support and supervision within an agency that is providing services to young people who demonstrate the impact of trauma and abuse, it may feel safer to avoid taking on a case than to engage with a situation that is poorly understood, poorly resourced and where there is little supervision in managing it.

In summary, either passing the case on or staying quiet about the existence of the problem might be easier for practitioners as opposed to trying to respond without adequate supervision and resources. If there is concern that your agency may be penalised after an inspection if the service is not seen to have met the needs of the young person, you might feel reticent about taking on a trafficking case. The implications of this are worrying: 'no action' might feel like a safer response than limited action.

Such an approach can result in those agencies that do have proven expertise in working with possibly trafficked young people being burdened with work that should actually be shared through multi-agency interventions. As noted by a voluntary sector provider:

> other agencies often use us as their extra resource . . . they will recognise the young people in care have gone missing and will let us know and we then spend all our time running around looking for things that we shouldn't be doing really.
>
> (Interview 26)

However, where multi-agency work was established, it had positive benefits:

> Working together with other professionals – the more that happens the better it is for everyone . . . that frees us to support the young person . . . it allows each professional to fulfil their specific role as best as possible . . . no one agency can do it on their own . . . collaborating and working together but also keeping their roles to an extent as well.
>
> (Interview 13)

In research by Burgoyne (2011), these positive experiences and the strengths and benefits of multi-agency working have been outlined. Burgoyne also suggests that there have been frustrations, confusions and difficulties in this work between agencies, such as inconsistencies around referral thresholds, tensions between agencies and discrimination against children not born in the UK.

We look in more detail below at some of the reasons why some agencies may feel ill-equipped or fearful of working with a young person who may have been trafficked, drawing on cases identified within the research of young people where health or education service practitioners recognised the young person as having been trafficked at the point of referral, as well as those practitioners who identified a trafficking trajectory after a number of years of intervention.

Noticing the indicators of 'being trafficked': health care practitioners

> If a child's brought in from a foreign country – never allowed out and told to get dinner ready every night and look after the baby – do they know [it isn't right]? Do they have that same deep down feeling that this isn't right? I don't think they do.
>
> (CS012)

> She came into the UK in 2004 . . . She was brought in for the sole purpose of being a domestic to look after the child, denied schooling . . .
>
> (CS010)

It is characteristic of traffickers to keep the trafficked young person hidden or invisible to health, education or other services. While some young people who have been trafficked are identified as such at the point of arrival in the UK, many remain hidden, often unaware of the full nature of the abuse they are experiencing. The 'wall of silence' and 'culture of disbelief' explained in chapter 5 mean that many remain in exploitative situations in the UK for many years before being identified as trafficked. Some, such as those working in cannabis factories or in domestic servitude, may be completely hidden from public and professional view, while others, such as those who might be sexually exploited or used for criminal activity, may be attending school, youth offending teams and/or using health services, yet without their experiences of exploitation being recognised or acknowledged.

The health problems experienced by the young people may be extensive, often including a combination of mental, sexual and physical health issues. Indeed, it is important to note that there were no cases in the research that were identified where a trafficked child or young person did not have a sexual, physical or mental health problem. For example, one practitioner noted:

> If they have been trafficked and they have not been looked after or cared for, then they may not have eaten properly, drunk properly, slept well. They certainly wouldn't have been given the immunisations they need, you know, all the basic things we take for granted.
>
> (Interview 2)

However, some health care practitioners noted that they lacked the experience to identify cases of trafficking. 'We aren't very good at identification of trafficking . . . I think we are in the early stages of identification' (Interview 25). One reason for this was that indicators appeared to be hidden from view.

She was taken to a sexual diseases clinic at some point for testing, but on the other hand, well I don't really know whether she could have been spotted at that time or not. But if she wasn't jumping up and down saying 'Help something's wrong here', it wouldn't necessarily alert anyone to it.

(Interview 30)

These quotations from a hospital-based nurse and a sexual health worker show some of the difficulties in identifying trafficked young people, suggesting that methods of identification could be improved. It was evident from our findings that many trafficked young people have a range of different health problems and that health practitioners need to be aware of the more subtle indicators of abuse, not relying on the young person being able to 'jump up and down' saying 'help'.

Of course, one of the dilemmas here refers back to the questions raised in chapter 2 and the way that work with adolescents involves recognition of the young person's agency (maybe they are saying that they don't want any help) while simultaneously acknowledging that they can be, and probably are, 'victims' of current or previous abuse. As noted, this is not easy as it requires sensitivity about the need to encourage the young person to be able to address the impact of the abuse on their behaviours while not undermining the young persons' sense of personal autonomy in the process. If the health worker above were responding to a child under 13 years of age (i.e. any sexual activity constituting statutory rape of a child under 13 under the Sexual Offences Act 2003), they would feel an unquestioned duty to intervene and instigate child protection procedures. When the young person is older and, once over 16, able to legitimately consent to sexual activity, stepping in becomes more difficult. Concerns about intruding on the young person's developing sense of agency and about perhaps alienating the young person from returning to the service mean that the practitioner might be hesitant in pursuing enquiries about suspected abuse.

As explored in more depth in chapter 2, this is a common question about how to negotiate with young people to ensure their child protection needs are maintained and understood while simultaneously ensuring that they do not feel undermined by statutory intervention: that they are given the opportunity to develop their own sense of agency and control over their situation. The good intention of securing the welfare of the young person is more easily rewarded in work with babies or younger children and can be wholeheartedly frustrated in work with adolescents who might reject service provider support, purporting to understand what is happening to them and how to manage. However, if the good intention of securing the welfare of the young person is abandoned as an ultimate aim, many young people will remain trapped in coercive and exploitative, often life-threatening situations.

The cases discussed below explore this a little further, referring to situations where young people were either unaware of the fact that they needed help; or unaware that help might be available; or actually asked for help. We try to draw out the complexities these different situations can present to various health care practitioners.

Health care: at the point of arrival

For many trafficked young people, health services may be the first point of contact they have with anyone who may be able to help them. Identification of some cases may occur at the point of the young person's arrival in the UK, where the hospital may be the first place to which a young person is referred.

> If any of them have immediate health needs we get them addressed right away, whether it's going straight to A&E or whether it's going to a health care clinic with a support worker . . . We've had that, we've had girls arrive at airport eight and a half months pregnant, who have gone straight to hospital . . .
>
> (Interview 13)

Sensitivity is needed in responding to the needs presented by the young people who may have little trust in, or experience of, contact with health care practitioners. For example: 'Sometimes physically they haven't been cared for in their own country . . . you almost have to have a medical that goes into everything which some young people would find very intrusive' (Interview 1); and also:

> She was about three months pregnant when she arrived in February . . . She was 14 . . . it was a result of rape . . . She claims it was part of the persecution essentially. She was raped because she was part of a particular minority clan . . . coming here to live with a man . . . I don't really know how well she knew him . . .
>
> (CS007)

Health care workers noted that reading the 'signs' or 'indicators' of having been trafficked can be complex, and require good observation skills. 'It's a lot to do with observation. It is how they present when you ask specific questions about their background and their journey. You see what their responses are like and their interaction with you' (Interview 13).

Health care: after having been in the country for a while

Other cases may involve health care workers being the ones who first identify the young person's experience of exploitation and abuse, sometimes
after the young person has been living in the UK for a number of years. In
the following case it was a health worker who first identified that the young
person had previously been trafficked into the UK for domestic servitude.
Indeed, the evidence recorded by the health workers provided the main
source of information for a later prosecution of the trafficker:

> She went through the hands of a number of local authorities who sent
> her back to her cousin . . . She was saying that he wasn't my cousin, I'm
> being trafficked, you know they're not treating me nicely . . . before
> finally presenting at a hospital and one of the medics picked it up
> . . . this was somebody that's been trafficked . . . but she's not disclos-
> ing half the information . . . We know a lot about her from medical
> examinations.
>
> (Interview 5)

And in a different case: 'Yes, and he had quite severe injuries . . . We were
very pleased because it was the hospital staff who alerted us to that' (Interview 26).

In other situations it became apparent that young people who had experienced exploitation for a while might be accessing health services as a means
of attracting attention to the abuse they were experiencing. For example, a
case was identified and reported by a health worker who felt that the young
person might be accessing the hospital as a way of escaping from her situation of abuse: 'although she was clearly unwell the hospital consultant felt
she might have exaggerated her illness in order to escape whatever situation
she was in' (CS001). This young person was using her initiative, trying to
communicate the pain that she was feeling but might have found impossible
to put into words. In this case, the excellent sensitivity of the consultant and
related hospital staff meant they looked beyond the surface to identify an
undisclosed history of trafficking for domestic servitude. Less sophisticated
responses could have perpetuated the often negative assumption that young
people may be attention seeking and time wasters, and discharged the young
person with no follow-up intervention.

One of the ways perpetrators exert control over young people is to prevent
them from accessing or using any service, including school and health care
services. The child will be prevented from registering with, or visiting, a GP
for fear that the abuse will be identified. In these situations, there was evidence of young people 'escaping' to access a 'walk-in centre' or 'accident

and emergency' to treat severe health problems. 'They walk into things like "walk-in centres" because they can't register with a GP so they use A&E and walk-in centres' (Interview 27). The young person might 'walk in' with a number of health problems that need attention. For example, one case file noted that a young woman 'dropped in' to a walk-in centre with:

- bruising to upper arm
- bruising to right eye which is sore when she looks to the right
- lesion to the eye, was pushed to the floor to be beaten and then couldn't see
- loss of consciousness, has flu and headache
- beaten with a fist several weeks ago
- been beaten three times before.

(CS006)

Research tells us that delayed disclosure of sexual abuse is common and young people may disclose indirectly through their actions, behaviours and non-verbal cues (Allnock 2010). They may also disclose abuse over time, gradually or incrementally, purposefully or through elicitation. Our study endorses this, suggesting that the trafficked young person may use a variety of methods to try to gain the attention of 'outsiders', trying to disclose the ongoing abuse that is hidden and protected 'inside' their daily activities. This may include exaggerating a physical medical problem in the hope that this will give them access to service providers or going to A&E or 'walk-in centres' when traffickers prevent their access to a GP.

Health care: identifying young people born in the UK trafficked for sexual exploitation

As with the identification of young people trafficked into the country from abroad, hospitals and health care staff also played an important role in identifying young people who were born in the UK (or who had lived in the UK for a substantial period of time, with UK citizenship) who might have been trafficked for sexual exploitation. Indeed, in noting the impact of human trafficking, the recent report from the government's Taskforce on the Health Aspects of Violence against Women and Children commented:

For many women who are effectively imprisoned in their home or community, seeing a health professional for urgent or routine treatment may provide the only opportunity they will have to seek help and to avoid coming to more serious harm.

(2010: 40)

It stated that 'it is clear that there is a lot of work to be done in order to raise awareness and for health services to respond to the needs of victims of harmful traditional practices and human trafficking'. This report offers advice to health care practitioners on identifying and supporting abused women who may have multiple health needs.

Our research noted similar concerns about the multiple health needs of trafficked young people. For example, worry was expressed about the physical and sexual health of this UK citizen who visited her GP: 'Concerns for young person as she was found to have blood poisoning, and concerns about drug use. She appears to be undernourished, anaemic and is reported to have numerous sexually transmitted diseases' (CS022). The concern noted by the GP led to a referral to children's services for an assessment of the young person's circumstances, which in turn led to identification of a history of sexual exploitation, of 'going missing' and of the young person being moved from one city in the UK to another for the purpose of exploitation. Similarly, two further cases were identified by health care practitioners following concern about the relationship between the child and her partner:

> has had second termination . . . was obtained without the knowledge of both her foster carer and the GP. In both instances appointments were made for young person at the hospital and she was taken there and collected by an adult male. The young person has reiterated that the father of her child is a 17-year-old but she was accompanied to the hospital by a male who was reported to be about 25 years.
>
> (CS 016)

Suspicions about the relationship between this young woman and the adult male were reported to children's services, and an assessment followed that identified sexual exploitation. Another second, and similar case, was of a young woman reported to children's services by a sexual health nurse from a sexual health clinic. The nurse was concerned that the young woman had a number of missed appointments. This helped identify the young person as 'formally' missing after previous concern about her health and well-being. 'Young person is not attending her medical appointments, she was due to meet with designated nurse but she did not attend this appointment' (CS025).

Our research showed that it was essential for sexual health workers to be aware of the indicators of trafficking, both of young people from abroad and of UK nationals moved around within the country, and to know what to do if they had concerns about a case. Both male and female trafficked young people in our research had experienced sexual health problems. While these problems were more common among those who had been trafficked for sexual exploitation, there was evidence of young people being trafficked for domestic servitude and then sexually abused and/or raped.

Those who had experience of working with trafficked young people, or who had received training on indicators of trafficking for sexual exploitation, noted that something as basic as the young person's age should raise concern.

> We've taken initiatives in the past in relation to young women who appear at sexual health clinics, especially if they're young. And take the view, 'Look, we've got to be interested in why this young woman is coming for contraceptives . . . she fell pregnant and attended the surgery to have pregnancy test done . . . Accompanied by white male in his mid thirties. Nurse suspected that he might be responsible for the pregnancy and described him as "being very much in control of the little girl". GP expressed concern regarding child's emotional well-being as she had previously taken an overdose.'
>
> (CS034)

This case was referred on for assessment through child protection procedures, the main indicators of concern being the age discrepancy between the young woman and the man who accompanied her, concern compounded by the fact that she was silenced by the man's presence. A situation where an adult talks for the young person was noted to be a strong indicator of abuse in situations of domestic servitude. A health practitioner noted that health visitors making home visits sometimes had suspicions: 'We have had cases where health visitors have gone into homes and there has been an unknown person with a child lurking around somewhere. It is just about being alert really' (Interview 27). Another professional emphasised the role health visitors can play in identifying possible cases of trafficking:

> Health visitors are very important in gathering that kind of information but often may not want to ask those questions. We had one child who a health visitor found wandering the streets. The child was naked and it was a real can of worms because, when we took them back ('home'), there were about five or six children living at that address all with different surnames and it seemed like a group of fathers looking after them. It was a very strange set-up. We need to know the histories of these children, it is very important.
>
> (Interview 25)

Similarly, a nurse designated to the LSCB made enquiries regarding the case noted below, linking pieces of the story together to reveal the extent of the abuse that the young person was experiencing while she was working in domestic servitude and being sexually exploited.

> We had a young woman who had been facilitated into the country . . . She was made pregnant by a foster carer's brother . . . then she was pregnant again within nine months and . . . in fact she took herself to the GUM [genito-urinary medicine] clinic and told a completely false story about herself and it was only because our designated nurse made a link with the GUM clinic that all the issues came together.
>
> (Interview 10)

As seen, practitioners from the range of health care services can play a crucial role in identifying a young person's history of being trafficked, including young people brought into the country from abroad and UK nationals trafficked for sexual exploitation.

Youth offending teams: identifying trafficked young people

Just as some young people may have approached health care services with the conscious or unconscious hope that their abuse might be recognised and stopped, so too may some young people commit offences as a call for help. This, alongside cases when young people have been trafficked into the country for work in the 'informal', criminal economy, may inappropriately bring the young person to the attention of police and youth offending team workers.

Practitioners in the youth justice system note evidence that some young people who have been trafficked become, either intentionally or otherwise, engaged in petty crime. Their involvement might result from coercion or force to commit offences on behalf of the abuser, from hunger, or from the desire to survive if they are 'on the run' after going missing. Alternatively, involvement in crime can be a method for the young person to gain the attention of professionals and may provide an opportunity for a history of having been trafficked to be identified. As noted by a youth offending team manager:

> we can get youngsters who will commit very minor offences to get noticed, as maybe a plea for help. So they may commit a minor shoplifting offence, come to the notice of the police and then hope that somebody is going to notice or find out what might have happened to them.
>
> (Interview 13)

In a similar vein, a case example was provided by a practitioner who, after work with a young person, realised that the child's shoplifting was an attempt to draw attention to her circumstances. The young person thought that if she were caught by the police, she would have to be taken away from the family for whom she worked in domestic servitude.

> She was staying with this lady and then went out shoplifting and was caught by the police. That's how she came to our attention. She had then been put into foster care and they noticed a man hanging around the address and that caused some concern . . . this guy was hanging around and was obviously waiting for her.
>
> (CS025)

As noted in chapter 2, the Sexual Offences Act 2003 specifies that children and young people coerced into sexual exploitation (which can involve being coerced into, or result in, committing offences) should be directed to child protection services, being worked with as victims of abuse. The offending behaviour of a sexually exploited young person should therefore be understood within the context of the exploitation and abuse (DCSF 2007). In this way, trafficked young people's behaviour, even if it involves criminal behaviour, should be seen in the context of the manipulation and abuse they receive from traffickers. This has long been argued by organisations such as ECPAT, CTAIL and the Refugee Council supporting young people who have been forced to work in cannabis factories (ECPAT UK 2010; Chandran 2011). Even if the young person is of the age of criminal responsibility and acknowledges an intention to offend, the offending behaviour should be understood in the context of abuse. As well as police being mindful of this, it is important that practitioners in youth offending teams are equipped to identify indicators of trafficking so that they too can understand and work with the offending behaviour in context.

While it is important to encourage practitioners in youth offending teams and related youth justice initiatives to be able to recognise histories of trafficking within their client group, it is also important to raise the bigger question of why victims of abuse are being criminalised at all. While interrelated, these two factors – how to recognise histories of trafficking and then how to understand why the criminal activity may result from being trafficked – are different. The details of how to achieve an understanding of both are beyond the remit of this book. Suffice it to say here that our research revealed different reasons for the young person being engaged with the youth offending teams or with health service providers. Sometimes the process of actively offending or actively exaggerating health problems was to seek attention in the hope that their abusive situation might be identified. This is an expression of the young person's agency. They are taking steps to try to address the problems they have and the circumstances they are in. If these steps are dismissed or resolutely questioned by practitioners, the young person's sense of agency will be undermined and they may not return to services for support. Worse still, they may despair and damage themselves further, or react by turning towards, rather than away from their abusers.

These issues take us back to the questions raised in chapter 2 about interpretations of, and work with, young people's agency: questions that call for a sophisticated practice that both enables young people to feel some control over their actions and ensures that they are also aware of the adult's role in safeguarding them from harm. The issues are explored further below in looking at the role of education services in identifying and supporting children who may have been trafficked.

Education and trafficked young people

Engaging trafficked children and young people within the school

Above we focused on the role of health care workers and youth offending team workers in identifying trafficked young people. Similarly, once trafficking is identified, the school can play an essential role in supporting the young person to integrate into a community and beginning to develop and achieve alongside their peers. It is important to note, however, that many trafficked young people are not on school rolls at all. They may be denied access to school by traffickers; they may have been introduced to a school but then their attendance has 'dropped off'; or they may be excluded because they have exhibited disruptive behaviours, many finding it hard to settle and overcome the impact of the abuse they have experienced.

Despite many problems in integrating into school, many trafficked young people actively seek an education as a route into a 'better life'. The way that the school culture and individual teachers respond to the challenges of helping a young person to integrate into the school has a significant impact on the young person's achievements in school. Essentially, effecting a successful integration requires complex multi-agency work. In particular, collaboration between education providers, interpreters and health service providers can provide essential support to the young person. As noted by a key worker: 'Education is very important . . . we provide a computer for the young person, home tutors, interpreters where necessary . . . I think that health support was very good '(Interview 28).

The Children Act 2008 specifies that a 'designated person' should be allocated from within the school staff team to oversee work with each looked-after child in the school (Children and Young Person Act 2008,

Part 2, section 20). This development recognises the importance of a good relationship between the young person and the school. It acknowledges that engagement with the young person and their sustained attendance at school is more likely if there is a particular staff member who is keeping the child in mind.

Our research showed the importance of the role played by the school and a specific 'designated person' for trafficked young people. The school provided support

> not just for education's sake in the early days, but so that we could have a structure to their life where they had somewhere to go. Otherwise they would just be so vulnerable, being chaotic and bored and easily picked up. So the whole structure was around keeping them safe and occupied and healthy.
>
> (Interview 6)

It also highlighted a number of cases where the young person was achieving at school, often as a result of coordinated support and multi-agency interventions. As noted in one case study, the young woman had

> started school in China when she was 7 years old and continued until she was 10 years old . . . She was not subject to any previous school exclusions . . . is on roll now and attending . . . Went to school every day without any problems, received a 'good progress award' certificate . . . Enjoys student life and appears to be achieving well. Took SATs and doing GCSEs – achieved a C in science, B in maths and A in art . . .
>
> (CS024)

Providing education to the trafficked young person outside the school environment

Not all young people who had been identified as trafficked were able to attend school. Many might have experienced such severe problems that it might have been perceived either as 'too late' to integrate them into the school, or 'too difficult' to achieve.

Undertaking a thorough assessment of the young person's needs and the suitability of a school to meet these needs was shown to be essential. Analysis of the case studies showed some tension between cases where young people wanted to attend school but agencies felt that they were not ready and put the referral 'on hold', while other cases suggested that the young person had been admitted to school without a full and proper assessment of their academic needs and ability to cope with the school environment.

Despite this, alternative 'out of school' contact with education providers through home tuition or referral to off-site or residential provision was noted as important as it provided a means of maintaining continued contact with the young person concerned.

For example, the following case shows a young woman who had been trafficked into the UK for sexual exploitation. Her sexualised behaviour was difficult to manage within the classroom environment, and was coupled with aggressive and destructive self-abuse. She was felt to be beyond the control of the school:

> In the UK living with her alleged father and uncle but not blood relative. Young person was not in education for three months until referral . . . Excluded from her secondary school due to behaviour problems, including disruption and sexualised behaviour to peers . . . Social worker states that mainstream education is not appropriate due to her behaviour problems . . . Looking into finding a therapeutic residential placement with education . . . Young person is a risk to male staff due to her past behaviour.
>
> (CS027)

The question about how sophisticated methods of intervention can support a vulnerable young person within the school environment while protecting both male and female staff is important (Luxmoore 2008). Although the young woman referred to in the case above demonstrated behaviour that was too difficult to manage within a mainstream school, she was entitled to accommodation in a safe place and to education provision. In some situations, placement in therapeutic residential units that provide education may be suitable.

Other cases also revealed particular behaviours that were extremely difficult for the school to manage. The young woman below, who had been trafficked into the country for domestic servitude and sexual exploitation, had been badly bullied when she was at school and had become pregnant. She was being temporarily educated through home tuition outside the school environment, and her intention was to continue at college after completing GCSEs and go on into higher education. The flexible approach of the authority in providing this home tuition was enabling her to hold on to her aspirations, despite having been made pregnant through an abusive relationship.

> Is being bullied at school because of her eye . . . Currently receiving home tuition . . . Happy in her foster placement and seems to have a good attachment with her foster carers. She has given birth to a

healthy baby girl and appears to be a caring mother, receiving support from a health visitor, wishes to resume her education and train as an accountant . . .

(CS034)

As noted, some young people were not deemed ready to engage with mainstream schooling. This meant additional preparatory interventions were needed to help them to develop some basic skills before they were able to manage referral to a school. In the situation below, an example of good practice showed children's services child protection workers, housing workers and education practitioners working together to help trafficked young people develop the skills and experience needed before they could integrate into mainstream schooling:

> peer group mentoring, we'd put them in a flat with someone else who spoke the same language who'd been here a bit longer . . . If there was a responsible sort of peer we'd get them to teach them how to do shopping and food and managing money . . . We started getting them to have little certificates: we'd teach them how to look after the flat and how to keep safe, how to telephone for the police, how to get health help, how to cook a simple meal and shop and their money . . . We had different sort of charts and when they were all ticked they proved that they had that part of independent living . . . We wouldn't let them move on until they'd reached the criteria.

(Interview 6)

In these cases, home tuition was considered the most supportive and appropriate method of enabling the young people to develop their education. While not ideal, as it separated the young person from their peer group, it enabled them to continue with education until they were ready to try to integrate into the school. Essentially, this depended upon close work between the home tutor, the health visitor, GP and child protection services.

For many trafficked young people it is language barriers that prevent integration into mainstream schooling and restrict access to continued education.

> On arrival, she was not in school . . . I mean they send them to English lessons so she'd need to get that before she got sent to mainstream school . . . They do sometimes voice their concerns [and] say 'I want to go to school', and we have to explain that 'You don't yet speak the language' . . .

(CS007)

Some practitioners were concerned that the amount of time needed to improve the young person's English so that they could attend school might result in the child being left behind the others in their peer group. This might mean that they had to join a class with young people who were younger than themselves. 'Education is a bit of a problem; getting them into schools in the appropriate year group – that's a big problem' (Interview 1).

Education practitioners who had worked with young people who had been trafficked from abroad were acutely aware of this problem, but invariably argued for integration into the school environment, even if it meant that the young person needed extra support classes outside the classroom and/or had to join a younger peer group. Practitioners with experience were concerned that if trafficked young people were 'lumped together' in off-site provision with the specific aim of improving their English before entry to mainstream school, they might metaphorically 'implode' upon themselves, their problems becoming the centre of attention. Many trafficked children were enthusiastic about continuing their education and did not necessarily want to be co-located with other vulnerable young people who had been trafficked. Also, there was concern that the site for their classes outside school may become known to and targeted by traffickers.

Whatever problems may exist with integration, it was deemed that the young person was safer inside the school than out. Rather than keeping the young person out of school until they have learnt English, one of the sites where the research was carried out ran the English language support work within the school. However, even here the practitioner was mindful that the young people might be encouraged into further exploitation through being grouped together in English language courses:

> [we] offer support [with] getting them into education . . . We do have projects that are in our schools . . . where they can work with other young people who have limited English . . . They are integrated into the mainstream school once they have picked up English as well . . . Also they can access counselling in the schools . . . We may need to look at more protection for some . . . If there is an ongoing investigation, we may not want them to be mixing with certain other groups of peers where they could be influenced . . . It's looking again at how all these different needs interlink with each other . . .
>
> (Interview 12)

As well as trying to facilitate language development within school, practitioners noted the important role that looked-after children nurses played in identifying and working with trafficking cases. '[We] developed a service within school nursing to provide a better service to our looked-after children' (Interview 2). Other school support staff felt confident in making referrals to a school nurse if they identified a problem, especially if the school advocated a multi-agency approach to supporting the young people:

> we've got a worker at the main secondary school who's actually been employed to support the Slovakian pupils . . . He's taken part in home visiting with us . . . he's been quite useful support . . . and because we're working as a multi-agency team now, if there were any medical needs we would be encouraging the school to refer to the school nurse.
>
> (Interview 17)

> If a teacher suspects that this child is trafficked, before it ever gets to me or to the team, it has to go through social services, because education automatically refer to social services . . . If it goes to a social worker who doesn't know much about trafficking, it may never get to the police.
>
> (CS011)

Education for the 16 to 18 age group

As outlined in chapter 1, a major concern identified by a number of practitioners was about what would happen to the young people as they approached 18. At this point they would be faced with the prospect of being returned to their country of origin. The build-up of anxiety about what was going to happen once they reached 18 was evident in the work with the 16 to 18 age group. The most utilised and temporary granting of the legal status of a trafficked child is that of Discretionary Leave. For those under the age of 17 years this often means that deportation – or 'administrative removal' – will occur at the age of 18.

One practitioner noted that the insecurity faced by the young people about their future makes it very hard for them to plan for their future education or career: 'While that process is going on they are in limbo, they don't know what's going to happen to them and they can't make plans for the future. It hinders their education' (Interview 17).

Many of the young people who had been trafficked into the country had settled into the UK, considering it to be their 'home'. In many cases, their knowledge of their country of origin was either confused (with little clarity of where they had come from or where they had been moved to over their time of being trafficked), too far away to remember, or unknown. Crucially, this included their knowledge of the education system, child protection systems or employment and welfare prospects in their country of origin.

While managing the uncertainties of this period is a specific problem for young people whose immigration status is unclear, it was also noted that the 16 to 18 age group of young people with UK citizenship who were trafficked within the UK for sexual exploitation often experience additional insecurities about their future. Many had diminishing contact with children's services as they progressed into adult services, often 'falling through the net' altogether. Once the young person reached the age of 16, and was perceived to take responsibility for consenting to sexual activity, it was often assumed that as young adults, they should manage their progression to adulthood alone. As noted in chapter 2, the resource pressures facing local authorities can mean that their service delivery is more specifically targeted towards younger children. A practitioner talked of what the Local Safeguarding Children Board responses might be:

> 'No, they're over 16 so they're not our responsibility.' The 16 to 18 age group is a massive problem for us . . . You're dealing with young police officers who perhaps don't know a lot about trafficking . . . you have to say 'Look, you need to tell them that they have a duty to care . . .'
>
> (CS015c)

Gathering evidence to prosecute traffickers

We have noted that health, youth justice and education workers have an important role to play in identifying and supporting young people who have been trafficked. We have noted that the interventions provided are best when delivered within a multi-agency framework (this point is developed further in chapter 7). We explore below the important role that police and other law enforcement agencies can play in this multi-agency framework, helping to work with practitioners to gather intelligence that could be used in prosecutions against abusers.

The Palermo Protocol (2000) definition of trafficking has three main strands: the 'act' of trafficking (for example, the recruitment, the transportation and the transfer of human beings); the 'means' of trafficking (the use of violence, threats, force, coercion); and the 'purpose' of trafficking (the form taken by exploitation, e.g. sexual exploitation, domestic servitude, forced criminality). Evidence to secure a successful prosecution for trafficking offences will probably be needed for each of the three strands within this definition.

The full range of practitioners from different agencies can help police and the Crown Prosecution Service, playing a central role in gathering intelligence that can be used as evidence to secure a prosecution. They also have a central role in working with the police to facilitate access to the young people if it is required in the process of securing a prosecution. The process of gaining information from young people that can be used in court is complex, often relying on a feeling of trust between the young person and practitioner interviewing them. The organisational processes for ensuring follow-up support with the young person throughout the painful process of reporting about the abuse need to be managed between the different collaborating professions.

For example, if a young person is admitted to hospital as an inpatient, it is possible that the hospital setting can become a 'safe place' for the police to interview them, gathering intelligence that can be used as evidence in respect to the 'means' used and potentially, the 'purpose' of having been trafficked.

> We had her medically examined at the children's hospital. She was seen by a forensic doctor and a paediatrician for both the forensic side of things and her health and well-being . . . tests for STDs and things were carried out . . . We also video interviewed her . . .
>
> (Interview 22)

If supported appropriately, the young person can feel secure in a ward where nurses and security staff are present in shifts, providing 24-hour cover. If it is possible for a positive relationship to be established between the designated 'social worker', the allocated police and the hospital staff, the young person can be supported to disclose evidence that could, in combination with hospital records, be intelligence used as evidence in court against an abuser. In addition, if the abuser were to see a coordinated strategy develop around the young person to protect them from further abuse, they may be discouraged from continuing contact with the child.

Essentially, the need for the young person to feel believed was argued to be at the core of helping to keep them feeling safe. Another case showed how interviews with the young person were conducted through collaboration between health workers, child protection workers and the police. In this case the young woman had been trafficked into the country for sexual exploitation. The young woman was interviewed by police when she was admitted to hospital:

> She was admitted to hospital late January 08, for a stomach virus. Hospital staff advised that she had possibly given birth before arriving in UK. Repeatedly raped when abroad . . . Clear during the interview conducted by police in January that she was anxious, and that her body language and hesitant answers indicated that she may have been withholding information that may have been upsetting to talk about.
>
> (CS 001)

Time was given to ensuring that the young woman felt safe and that understandable explanations were given to her about the different roles the workers would play in helping her to move on, once she had recovered from her physical injuries. The information that the young woman was then able to provide to the designated social worker, police and health care staff was, alongside evidence from the medical examination, used in a subsequent successful prosecution against the traffickers who abused her.

As the recent prosecutions against perpetrators who have sexually exploited children and young people have shown, coordinated police activity in collaboration with NGOs, health and education service providers can result in successful convictions which prevent further harm and abuse (Jago *et al.* 2011). Case studies examined for our research showed that where police were trained and resourced to identify and work with trafficked young people, the gathering of evidence against abusers improved. There was a realisation that multi-agency working with the police enhanced the opportunity for the young person to be and feel safe.

The following case illustrates this. A young woman had been trafficked into the country and, following a period of sexual exploitation, escaped, running straight to a police station. As the particular police force had been funded, trained and resourced to identify and respond to cases of trafficking, they were able to provide immediate support to the young woman and, while making appropriate referrals to support agencies, pursue the gathering of intelligence immediately.

> City centre police stations aren't always open 24 hours so you've basically got a distressed 15-year-old who couldn't speak a word of English banging on the door of the police station . . . Normally with a situation like this, with a rape investigation, you've got specially trained officers who do the interview. We were quite fortunate with the funding we'd got from an operation . . . Yeah, she was quite fortunate.
>
> (CS015)

In another case, the police were able to act on suspicion that a young person with UK citizenship, born and brought up in the UK, was being trafficked within the UK. They worked with others to support her through the interview process and court case. As there had been an active operation focusing on sexual exploitation, funding, training and resources were made available

> Staff at the residential unit found £670 in the girl's room and she said this bloke had lent it to her . . . So the police went and spoke to her . . . they were saying it was evident she was infatuated with him . . . beside

being 15 and she agreed to be video interviewed . . . There was one male that got ten years for anal and vaginal rape . . . five others were charged with offences . . . She was really brave actually. She gave evidence and she was commended in the end by the judge as to how brave she was giving evidence . . . But then we did have operation experience and so the police were involved with that as they had the dedicated time to do that . . . The police stuff was really ongoing and looking at serving abduction letters on whoever they could find, so there was quite a lot of police activity and things like the residential unit were actually seeing if they could get any car registration numbers that were seen.

(CS020)

In some other situations, however, there was worry as to whether resources were available to follow the movement of a young person within the UK: 'We did have a problem that she was trafficked from one police region to another and that information is not communicated and there was a lack of resources to spend time joining up that investigation' (CS016). There was awareness that, when faced with a complex case involving a number of young people involved with a large criminal network, considerable policing resources are needed: 'the real problem is that there is insufficient policing of these criminal networks' (CS017).

Despite this, as seen in the cases above, where policing was resourced and staff trained, there were examples of very successful interventions where the young person was safeguarded from further abuse:

There is an ongoing investigation with trafficking and the two people that they suspect are being charged . . . Working with the police, they've been excellent, really good, come to see the young person again and again, so that they're familiar with them and trust them.

(Interview 13)

Multi-agency work in supporting the young person through the process of managing the prosecution meant involving solicitors who had a working knowledge of the issues facing trafficked young people. Access to a supportive and informed solicitor, or to an appropriate legal adviser, could help the young person understand their rights if they were taking a case to court:

got a solicitor for her defence . . . We formed a very strong working relationship with social services legal team as well . . . we applied to the judge for the disclosure of her account in the family court . . . because obviously family court stuff is private . . .

(CS010)

One local area had specifically selected and trained a group of solicitors to help them manage their work with trafficked young people:

> We've learnt to select a certain group of solicitors that have got experience in trafficking now. You gather those little bits of anecdotal information that say, 'Well, this one was really good on that case', and about joining cases together.
>
> (CS033)

Importantly, as well as advising the young people, solicitors play an essential role in acting as sounding boards for practitioners: 'We know that she had a legal representative, because they made a representation on her behalf, and we've also consulted with them when she went missing' (CS004).

Conclusion

This chapter has explored the difficulties faced by practitioners in identifying and responding to the needs of the young person. It has noted that without training, resources and support, practitioners may be fearful of engaging with a trafficked young person, passing the referral on as a 'hot potato' rather than trying to engage and finding that they are poorly equipped to achieved expected 'outcomes'. If the young person has committed offences, while youth offending team workers may have a statutory duty to work with them, they are in a particularly pertinent position to highlight the relationship between the young person's experience of abuse and their offending behaviours.

Health practitioners, particularly in accident and emergency units and in sexual health services, have particular opportunities to identify abuse experienced by trafficked young people. Indeed, trafficked young people may specifically approach these services with the conscious or unconscious wish that their experience of exploitation is detected. It is important to note here that children's mental health workers carry a similar responsibility, and this is explored further in chapter 7. While many trafficked young people may be very keen to attend school to enhance their education, particular attention needs to be placed on managing their integration, supporting them within the school environment. When it is not possible for them to attend school, our research suggests that home tuition and ongoing educational support can help the young person to remain optimistic about achieving some educational outcomes. If agencies such as youth offending teams, health and education are able to work together with police and child protection staff, intelligence can be gathered that can eventually be used in a prosecution against abusers.

In summary, proactive interventions led through multi-agency working to support trafficked young people, with regular supervision of the staff engaged in the work, can help to build positive, trusting relationships between practitioners and the young people concerned. To achieve genuine multi-agency work where intelligence is shared, skills need to be combined for the benefit of the child. Importantly, this means welfare and justice agencies working closely together throughout the different developmental stages of the child or young person.

In chapter 7 we continue to focus on the importance of multi-agency working with trafficked young people. While we continue to stress the need for all agencies to be able to identify and support trafficked young people, we particularly focus on specialist services that are essential to the development of the trafficked young person's well-being. That is, while generic services underpin good practice, specialist services are needed for particular purposes. All need to be underpinned by multi-agency working practices.

7 Specialist services

Securing safety at the point of arrival

As seen in chapter 6, our research noted that universal, mainstream service providers need to be able to both identify and engage with suspected cases of trafficking. That said, the trauma, abuse and displacement that many of the young people have experienced, either before or after entry to the UK, create specialist needs that require particular dedicated services staffed by specifically trained practitioners. Although all universal services need to be aware of and be able to respond to the needs of young people who have been trafficked, they may not be equipped to manage the specific needs presented by some cases where language barriers and past and ongoing trauma and abuse have a severe impact on the young person's capacity to engage.

In this chapter we explore the need for services to be available first and foremost for any young person at the point of entry to the country, including access to a place of safety with an allocated key worker from statutory children's services prior to any questions emerging about 'immigration status' or 'age assessment'. Central to all these requirements is the need for the development of secure and trusted relationships that can be modelled against abusive and exploitative relationships. As such, we advocate a 'relationship based' model for the development of interventions with trafficked young people. We look at the need for the initial placement to be 'front loaded', with significant time and resources given to securing the young person's immediate safety as they begin to settle into the placement. We look at when and why young people may 'go missing' from their placement, and explore how a relationship based approach may enable the young person to feel that someone is thinking about them, or worrying about them, while they are missing, something that might encourage them to make contact with the carer or, indeed, eventually return.

Case study: Rosa's story

Rosa arrived in the UK in June 2007 from China when she was 14½ years old. In initial age assessment she was thought to be 18 years old as she had been told to say this by the agent who brought her into the country. The amount of debt this agent claimed from Rosa remains unknown.

When she first arrived she was placed in accommodation close to the airport, where there was no Chinese-speaking worker or interpreter. While in this accommodation she met another Chinese young woman who said she would help her. She was then taken to a man and forced to work in a brothel for seven months. She managed to escape. She returned to the original accommodation as she had been able to hold onto a leaflet with the address and map that had been given to her. Importantly, key information on the leaflet was translated into a number of different languages, including Chinese.

When interviewed, she stated that 'bad things' had happened to her in the UK but would not provide any further details. There were physical signs on her body of having been tied up. Some information was provided to the police about the people who held her but, to date, very little is known about her experiences.

Services available at the point of entry to the country: helping the young person to feel safe

Rosa's case raises a number of issues about responses to trafficked young people at the point of entry to the UK. The question of an appropriate approach to undertaking age assessments and the need for an immediate place of safety emerge, as does the need for interpreters to help Rosa to understand the situation she finds herself in. Questions regarding age assessment and a place of safety are addressed below, while questions of access to specialist and trained interpreters follow in chapter 8. In this section we address the requirements that secure the safety of a trafficked young person at the point of entry to the UK.

Age assessment: an immigration or child protection issue?

Rosa was encouraged by the agent who brought her into the country to say that she was 18 so that she was diverted from child protection interventions where statutory services ask detailed questions, following established assessment protocols, about her circumstances (DCSF 2007). With Rosa posing as 18 years old, the agent would aim to bring her into the country as an adult friend or relative and then later place her in a brothel. The agent is taking a risk here as Rosa may be deported as an adult seeking illegal entry to the country.

However, the work on age assessment at point of entry suggests that sometimes immigration issues may precede concern over the welfare of the child, despite comprehensive guidance on proposing the reverse (DCSF 2007). Rosa was age assessed at the point of entry to be over 18, although when this was challenged by children's services she was placed in local authority care, from where sadly she later disappeared.

Disputes about the age of the young person at the point of arrival can be disturbing and intrusive, undermining any confidence the young person may have at the very point when they may be most vulnerable. Indeed, *When Is a Child Not a Child?* published by the Immigration Law Practitioners' Association confirms that:

> the problem of age disputes is linked to prevailing cultures of cynicism and disbelief among immigration officers and some social workers . . . There is a potential conflict of interest between the requirement of social service departments to undertake age assessments and the obligation to provide services to children in need . . . and . . . the current approach to age disputes and the process of age assessment is high-risk, costly and does not deliver high-quality outcomes for the Home Office, social services departments or separated asylum seeking children.
>
> (Crawley 2007: 1)

As noted, questions of age dispute should not come ahead of ensuring the young person's safety. This was endorsed by a number of practitioners: 'It is mainly around keeping them safe at the beginning' (Interview 4); 'they've got to feel safe before they can address any of these issues . . . before they can be examined by people' (Interview 5).

One interviewee noted that they are required to consider the need for age assessment, but confirmed that this came after ensuring the young person's safety:

> The first thing is safety. They need to feel safe . . . We always did initial assessments . . . but this was followed within usually two or three days but not more than a week by a planning meeting, when we'd have an interpreter present.
>
> (Interview 6)

Findings from a programme of expert consultation involving 285 organisations and individuals on therapeutic interventions reinforce this. It was found that intervention and service provision structured around a 'victim' centred and multi-agency approach (Itzin *et al.* 2010: 77) was considered to be the optimum stance in relation to child, adolescent and adult 'victims'/ 'survivors' of sexual exploitation, prostitution, pornography and trafficking. Essential to this is managing the tensions, identified earlier, in supporting a young person to acknowledge their victim status while engaging with services to advance their resilience, self-determination and well-being. We explore this below with particular focus on the immediate need to protect the young person from harm at the point of entry to the UK and throughout the initial process of settling into safe accommodation.

Securing a feeling of safety upon arrival

> She needs to stay in a safe, secure and emotionally warm environment to be able to grow and develop and gain self-care skills.
>
> (CS003)

> [I]t is not only that she is well or that she is healthy emotionally, but that she is safe. This is the first baseline to achieve.
>
> (CS027)

We have looked at the need for the young person's welfare to precede any intrusive questioning about their age, country of origin or possible future intentions. Inherent in this child-centred position is the need for the young person to begin to feel safe, and for them to have the groundwork laid for establishing some trust in professionals and confidence that they do not intend to harm them further. As already noted elsewhere, if the young person's previous experiences have been of adults in authoritative positions being abusive and untrustworthy, securing a position of trust and a feeling of safety will take time, requiring sensitivity and care.

Central to this was helping the young person to understand what they were being asked and why. While we look later in chapter 8 at the role that specialist interpreters can play in effecting this understanding, practitioners in our research explained that it was important to try to ensure that wherever possible the young person was aware that children's services had their best interests at heart, and that the young person would not be pressurised to disclose information that they did not understand or feel able to talk about. As such, it was considered appropriate to ensure the young person was allowed to take their time to disclose information about their experiences.

> If you've got a trafficked young person the most important thing is to reiterate the trust of social services, and that we are separate from the immigration and the police. Because we have to remember they've just come from being interviewed by immigration . . . a lot of that stuff's going to come out much further down the line than in the beginning . . . More of this stuff emotionally comes out once they've settled, once the sort of immediate crisis need's over . . .
>
> (Interview 13)

Young people's feeling of security with their legal status will be intricately bound up with their feeling of safety; that is, they cannot begin to feel safe if they think they are going to be deported back to unknown danger or returned to traffickers. The young person may be so frightened or displaced that they are unable to engage in any meaningful dialogue about their well-being.

> Some of them don't want to see a doctor or a GP. They aren't concerned about STIs or STDs, they want to know what their right to stay here is, and if they are at risk of being deported or removed . . .
>
> (Interview 17)

The above confirms that it may take a long time before the young person begins to feel safe and therefore a long time before they are confident enough to disclose experiences of abuse. Indeed, many young people's experiences may result in them not feeling safe for years, or even a lifetime. At the point of arrival, the young person may not be able to identify, understand or describe feelings of fear, displacement or pain they are experiencing. It is likely that the young person will be in a state of crisis, tired from travel (often accompanied by violence and abuse) and unable to understand the situation they are in. They will struggle to keep their experience in perspective and may find it impossible to think about, or certainly describe, their current or medium and long-term needs with clarity and appropriate consideration.

For example, one interviewee who had worked with young people at the point of their arrival into the country noted that 'they're just so frightened' (interview 10), while another noted:

> they're often either completely silent or tell you a different story . . . When they are told by a lot of people . . . that we're not to be trusted, it's a big barrier to overcome . . . They [the traffickers] will often say to the young person before we get to meet them 'Don't tell social services anything' and they all have a very common story, you know. They can't remember anything.
>
> (Interview 13)

Another noted that the young person may be repeating a script their trafficker has taught them to recount. This may, in itself, be an indicator of being trafficked. Noting the power of the trafficker, this practitioner suggests that the true experiences of the young person may be hidden under an instruction to say that they don't remember, or that they have been abandoned by an agent: 'their stories are all very similar, basically they're identical the stories – 'I got on a plane', 'I don't remember where I got here from', 'The agent left me at the airport' – they're all exactly the same' (Interview 6).

Alternatively, the young person may have no idea where they have come from, being genuinely unable to answer the basic question of 'where is your home and family?' Notes from a case study analysis show that a young person may indeed be completely confused and may not know where they have been, or even where they were originally from if they have been in the UK for several years unaccompanied: 'and he'll never know where he comes from, which is sad' (CS004).

The above suggests that an essential feature in helping the young person to feel safe at the point of arrival is to allow them time to settle and to build trust with the agencies that are there to help them.

Keeping the young person 'in mind': relationship based thinking

Recognising all these complex issues of how and why a young person may be able to begin to feel safe, practitioners noted the need for a dedicated, specialist trained staff member to be available to the child at the point of their arrival. There has been much discussion about the appropriateness of the allocation of a 'guardian', which we return to in more detail below. The allocation, or not, of a guardian should not excuse the relevant children's services from their responsibility to allocate a key worker to oversee all management of statutory services, placements and any court processes that may emerge as the child settles and discloses information. That is, statutory children's services should provide the young person with a 'key worker'.

This 'key work' approach is supported by relationship based thinking, a strand of social work theory developed from psychodynamic approaches which advance the importance of a secure and trusted relationship as a premise for significant interventions with those needing support (Luxmoore 2008; Howe 1998). Advocated by both Laming (2009) and Munro (2011), the approach argues that modelling 'good' relationships provides different experiences and expectations from the 'bad' abusive relationships the young person may have experienced. The actual experience of a good enough relationship, which is not abusive and holds the needs and interest of the young person at its centre, provides a grounding for the young person to move on, expecting support and care from future relationships, rather than expecting abuse and neglect.

> from what we have learnt it's constantly having someone, like a key worker, building that trusting relationship with the child to take them through, not just dismantling all that these men are doing, in terms of the so-called brainwashing, and then making them realise what exactly [a] positive relationship means to building that confidence in them to be able to stand up to these men and co-operate with the police and go through with the prosecution.
>
> (Interview 24)

Although resource intensive, this approach has been deemed to hold long-term benefits as (a) it helps to ensure the engagement of the young person, preventing repeat episodes of going missing and returning to abusive situations, and (b) it can provide a model for future relationships that prevent further abuse and therefore further continued need for intervention.

It has been argued that a guardian may take this role, providing consistency and support to the young person throughout their developing trajectory. NGOs such as ECPAT UK, the Refugee Council and the NSPCC have long argued that trafficked young people should be allocated a guardian at the point of entry to the UK. This person should remain as guardian with responsibility for monitoring all developments in service delivery throughout the young person's future. The argument is that the level of statutory, professional support provided to young people who are victims of trafficking varies widely and in some cases is inadequate. Even when a young person is looked after (under the Children Act 1989) there is an allocated social worker from the authority that holds *loco parentis*, meetings between the young person and the social worker may be too infrequent and the core child protection system may not be designed to fully understand or meet the specific needs of trafficked young people. That is, the guardian provides stability and continuity in the way that supportive parenting may provide a consistent sounding board to any other young person. Proposals for developing a framework for allocating guardians to young people who have entered the country as refugees and/or unaccompanied minors, whether through trafficking, smuggling or other means, are currently being considered and worked on.

Even if the guardianship system is advanced, our research suggests that this should not replace the allocation of a key worker from statutory services. The essential finding from our work was that, whether or not a guardian had been allocated, the children's services needed to allocate a 'key worker' to the young person to work with them throughout transitions and hold them in mind: 'and I suppose when you look at resources, the thing that you need is somebody that's pulling all that together, that's saying "This is what I'm doing, can you do this, can you do that?"' (Interview 20).

To illustrate the point further, it is helpful to refer to a situation where a local authority child protection worker spoke of a 16-year-old young woman who had been brought into the country when she was 10 years old. Following a number of private foster care breakdowns, she had been placed with a local authority specialist foster carer, with whom she developed a trusting relationship. She started to disclose information about the way that she had been trafficked within the country. However, the foster carer found it difficult to manage the young woman's eating disorder, which escalated as the police became involved in the case:

> when police try and contact her in the first place and make these video recordings and take the statements . . . this child was exhibiting suicidal tendencies, she had eating disorder – anorexia and all that. When she was moved into a psychiatric institution, all they were trying to treat was how they could make her eat . . .
>
> (Interview 21)

The statutory children's services key worker allocated to oversee the work with this case was able to maintain the important connection between the young woman and the police as she disclosed intelligence, while supporting the foster carer, who was managing the young woman's hospital appointments and admissions. At the same time, the key worker was working with the young person's school to maintain contact with the school staff member designated to oversee work with the child as required by the Children Act 2008. Through this relationship between the key worker and the school staff member, it was possible to maintain accurate and ongoing information sharing, enabling the young person to return to school following return from psychiatric care.

Two more examples of different young women who had been trafficked into the country for domestic servitude develop this point. The first young woman had been placed with a local authority foster carer after being removed from a situation of domestic servitude. She had been repeatedly raped by a man in the household where she was working. The allocated key worker noted that support was needed not only for the young woman but for the foster carer with whom the young woman was placed:

> We had one girl conceal a pregnancy for a good while, and I was saying we really ought to get her to a doctor just to get her checked over, you know a medical assessment. But she was just very, very scared. And

the foster carer was having terrible trouble getting her to undress for the shower and things like that, just because she was so scared . . .

(Interview 25)

The second young person had been recently removed from domestic servitude and was collaborating with her foster carer and key worker to take a case out against those who abused her. The key worker was faced with the task of trying to explain to the foster carer why the young woman had not run away from the family who abused her:

> yes, she had a key to the house, but I think that . . . if you were to allow your daughter to come and go freely, that would be a child who has a social network, because she goes to school and maybe has after-school clubs etc. etc. A domestic, to give them the key to the door . . . you know, she had no social networks, she had no friends other than the house owner . . . And defence barristers will always say 'Well, you know, why didn't you run away?' But if you put yourself in that child's position . . .

(CS011)

The key worker noted that she was not only explaining why the young woman had not run away before, but also why, now, living in a safe home with a carer who was offering support, the child was agoraphobic. The carer was working sensitively with the child who stayed in her room and did not want to leave, but needed the key worker's support to understand and manage the behaviour over the long term.

In essence, a designated, trained and supported child care key worker is needed to help the trafficked young person understand and manage the transitions they move through, and to help the carer in providing accommodation to cope with the pressures while installing some sense of 'normality' in the young person's life.

> So I think they need to feel safe and they need to know that their health needs are taken care of, and you know, one of the old-fashioned child protection things . . . when you did child protection medicals you'd reassure the child that they weren't horribly damaged or diseased.

(Interview 10)

Key worker role in gathering evidence to disrupt and prosecute abuser(s)

The key worker also plays an essential role not only in supporting the young person but also in helping to establish a trust that might eventually lead to the gathering of evidence that can be used for a prosecution of alleged traffickers. This echoes findings on effective methods of gathering evidence to protect young people from sexual exploitation (Jago and Pearce 2008; Jago *et al.* 2011) which advocate a four-stage strategy: 'identification of' and 'engagement with' the young person in order to effect 'disruption' and 'prosecution' of the abuser(s). It is recognised that the disruption and prosecution of the abuser(s) is very unlikely to happen without identification of and engagement with the young person, and that consistency in care is essential to the engagement process. With a carer, a key worker can help to gather information about the nature of the abuse which could be used as evidence in a later prosecution of the offender. For example, in this case where the young person was provided with therapeutic interventions coordinated through the foster care placement and the specialist foster carer was supported by a statutory key worker to manage the complex issues of disclosure, a successful prosecution was secured:

> We have had success with prosecution, that's the only case that we think is successful, was a foster home where the child was given therapeutic care. So that foster parents only take one child at each time and they offer therapeutic care. That did help the child, see through what was happening . . . and she went through the criminal justice process and those people were committed . . .
>
> (Interview 24)

Understanding 'going missing' during the settling in process

As noted in chapters 1 and 2, research has shown that a disproportionate number of trafficked young people go missing, many immediately at the point of arrival into the country (DCSF 2007).

> They've presented at the Home Office and said they've been trafficked by an agent to come into the country and . . . [we've] put them in a foster placement, and the following morning they've gone and left the placement . . .'
>
> (interview 12)

Evidence from interviews with practitioners and from case study analysis undertaken for this research suggests that the 'going missing' and 'running away' behaviour may not be an informed, all-knowing rebellious act of the young person concerned, but can be the result of coercion and entanglement in an abusive relationship or the result of a confused state of mind. Our research suggested that the initial few weeks of a young person's experience in placement were of paramount importance. For this reason we explored the concept of 'front loading' the placement experience.

'Front-loaded' intensive intervention

This 'front loading' approach means that during the first month the placement provides intensive support and monitoring of the young person (to be reviewed at the end of that period) by the trained, specialist care provider and allocated key worker. 'Front loading' may mean removing mobile phones, implementing curfews, accompanying the child on visits or trips outside the home and monitoring activities taking place within the home. Although this may appear to be limiting a child's freedom, and perhaps as somewhat draconian and contrary to the advancement of the young person's rights, it provides traffickers intent on retrafficking the young person with a clear message that the young person is being monitored and looked after. It is also a clear message to the young person that what happened to them before is wrong and unacceptable, and that the intention now is to keep them safe from this point onwards. They learn that they are important, worth caring for and are being protected. Central to the success of this approach is in helping the young person to understand that the 'front loading' is integrated into a longer term plan with a phased approach to enable them to move on safely.

The rationale for intensive front loading became apparent when data were gathered from interviews and case studies. For example, one practitioner identifies how the impact of organised crime changes the nature of placement requirements:

> I think that also in the local authority the blanket view is 'OK, well this child is looked after by us now so they're going to be safe.' And that's not necessarily the view and you know, with organised crime like this, that the child can be looked after, almost housed by foster carers, but when that child's leaving the house . . . what does that mean for the young person? I think they can still be at a huge amount of risk even if they are looked after.
>
> (Interview 28)

Not only could the traffickers target a location known for emergency placement of displaced young people, but the young people themselves could have an adverse influence on each other:

> There are no locks or bars, so the child can come and go as they wish and it's very easy for people to contact them underground . . . There are

several kids there all from one or another country, they would talk to each other and even if the kid hadn't been trafficked in the first place, one kid might put them in touch with traffickers. I think it is difficult as a local authority to have 'safe homes' because there are so many ways of contacting people.

(CS027)

If the young person is placed in a residential care home, it was noted that immediate 24-hour cover and supervision are essential. While some young people might inadvertently introduce others to harm or might be abducted, others are intent on 'escape', either to return to their traffickers to whom they owe money, or because they are following previous instructions, or, in some cases, because they feel an attachment or even 'love' towards those who have abused them. Alternatively, some young people felt that running away gave them some control over a situation that they did not understand. They would often take extreme measures to run from the accommodation they were given. A practitioner voices concern that the young person might go missing if the carers are not present throughout the day and night:

What they would do was jump out of the window, so now we've put them on the first floor, just to prevent that very thing – jumping out of the window and legging it in the early hours of the morning . . . If they're coming in on an 8 o'clock flight and they're being placed kind of 10 o'clock, 11 o'clock at night, if you can stop them going at three in the morning out of their window, by getting a member of staff in there the next day, beginning to start making a relationship with them, then maybe they won't go. But some of them still go after 24 hours you know, the next opportunity . . . the first opportunity that they get of having the front door and they're out . . .

(Interview 29)

Another noted with desperation: 'I've sat there for two hours with a young person saying 'These are the risks, please don't abscond' and then next day they've absconded' (Interview 13).

The important issue arising from the above is the acknowledgement that 'getting a member of staff in there the next day, beginning to start making a relationship with them' might mean that the young person could be prevented from running. Returning to the model of 'relationship based thinking' explored above, we see how a supported and trained designated carer allocated at the point of arrival with powers to intervene to protect the young person might make it possible for a relationship to be developed with the child or young person:

then, when she went to the specialist foster carer, she was one to one with her, that was her sole role, she didn't have any other jobs and she was just destined to look after the young girl until she was enrolled in the local college.

(CS015)

We noted earlier in the chapter that one of the immediate problems in securing the safety of a trafficked young person may be in supporting them to understand that they have been victims of abuse, and that to secure their safety they may have to have some of their basic rights infringed. This is hard in practice when, on the one hand, the desire is to secure safety and prevent repeat episodes of going missing and, on the other hand, the desire is to bond with the young person, to establish a positive relationship with them and to begin to support them in developing their own initiatives. The research shows that to manage this balance, practitioners and their supporting managers may have to take decisions that the young person may not immediately understand to be in their best interests. This may involve placing the young person in a placement away from their immediately identified 'home'.

Choosing the location of the placement

We have noted how securing a positive relationship between the key worker, carer and young person may help to prevent episodes of going missing, or at least help the young person to feel that they are being held in mind while they are away. Another proposal advocated by practitioners with experience of working with trafficked young people was that the initial placement should be unknown to traffickers. Although this may not be the young person's immediate choice, it recognises the aggressive approach traffickers will take to identifying and retrafficking young people they have previously 'owned'. The following two quotes note different practitioners' concerns for safety as they recognise that the young people will be targeted by traffickers after being accommodated.

She is a young girl trafficked to the UK by relatives and she was abused sexually and physically and locked in a brothel for two years . . . Needs to be in an environment with a lot of emotional support outside the city. She is afraid that she will bump into traffickers here . . . She needs to be placed in a safe foster placement where she is not having a risk to meet the trafficker.

(CS003)

I think we could probably do with some accommodation which is more, I don't know . . . safe and kept confidential. If you've got a destination where all the traffickers know . . . it's easier for them to go and pick them up.

(Interview 9)

Some practitioners were mindful that if trafficked young people were placed in the same accommodation together, the accommodation could become a target location for those who wanted to retraffic them: children could be placed at further risk if they were located in accommodation that was commonly used for a number of trafficked or other vulnerable children:

They would need very high levels of security; they wouldn't be mixing trafficked with other vulnerable young people. The major risk factor is that if you simply lump one group of very vulnerable young people with another it makes a situation worse.

(Interview 17)

In some situations it was felt that the child needed to be placed out of the borough to secure their safety:

often when children are given safe accommodation in other areas, which means taking them away from where the abuse is happening, [this] has helped . . . far enough away where it is not very easy for the child to come out and just take a train back . . . It's the control that these men have on them . . . Care home staff, they say 'Oh, we are helpless . . . We see these men outside the care homes, waiting in their cars and picking up young girls and we are still unable to do anything.

(Interview 24)

I can think of one young woman who couldn't stay in [name of area] . . . Because her abductors were still roaming around [there] . . . and she was terrified and obviously, in that case, we moved her out of the borough.

(Interview 10)

Although it was recognised that out of borough placements could be disruptive for the young person's schooling, or engagement with recreational or health service provisions, they might be necessary as a respite, interim measure if a young person was being relentlessly targeted.

These problems of protecting the young person through provision of safe accommodation, both in and out of borough, are explored further by

NGOs such as the British Association for Adoption and Fostering. There has recently been a stronger focus on the need for appropriate supported accommodation for trafficked and sexually exploited young people (Brodie *et al.* 2011), The UK Department for Education is currently funding a programme run by Barnardo's to pilot and evaluate a scheme offering trained and supported foster care accommodation to young people who have been trafficked and/or experienced child sexual exploitation. Despite this more recent acknowledgement of the specific accommodation needs of trafficked children, it is still not unknown for trafficked children and young people to be placed in bed and breakfast accommodation, in partially or unsupervised residential accommodation or with unsupported and untrained foster carers. This is condemned as bad practice (DCSF 2007). Practitioners noted the harm that such accommodation arrangements can cause, with the placement adding to the risks faced by the young person, leading to repeat episodes of going missing and lost opportunities to gather evidence against the traffickers who have abused the child.

What is clear is that local authorities intent on securing the safety of the trafficked young person will need a portfolio of placement types and access to trained, supported and specialist foster carers who can work with an allocated key worker to advance the young person's safety. The point made throughout a number of the interviews was that in planning accommodation for children who had been trafficked (whether it involved trafficking into the country from abroad, or the trafficking of UK nationals), there needs to be a conceptual shift, moving policy and practice away from accepting that the existing local authority accommodation for looked-after children or young people will suffice while recognising that it will be essential to create a genuine 'place of safety', ideally with specialist, trained and supported carers.

Training for foster carers, or residential care home staff, needs to equip them to:

- understand and manage the risk that traffickers will intimidate children and foster/care home staff;
- help prevent the abduction of the children concerned;
- help prevent the child from going missing;
- work with other related practitioners, including police if they are engaged, or about to engage in an operation against the traffickers;
- help the child to understand that they need to trust and work with foster/care home staff in order to stay safe;
- enable the child to understand their legal and immigration rights;
- help the child to begin to think about and identify problems with their emotional and physical and sexual health needs;

- support the child to incorporate the experience of specialist provision within their everyday lives (e.g. therapeutic support, sexual and physical health checks, attendance at special education such as Learning English courses);
- help the child to resettle, and to engage with mainstream universal services, particularly education and health;
- help the child to manage their own emotional development as disclosure of previous abuse takes place, and to disclose, where possible, details that would help to secure evidence against those who trafficked them.

The basic training needs listed have been shown by practice and research to be essential to prevent repeat episodes of going missing and to 'hold' the child during the initial stages of establishing a secure living environment (Fursland 2009). The accommodation provided to the child, the 'place of safety', relies on them having a safe relationship with a trained and responsible adult carer. This carer cannot support the child on their own. They need ongoing access to the designated child protection 'key worker' who is managing all other aspects of the case. It was argued in one site for our research that this worker should report regularly to the Local Safeguarding Children Board (or its trafficking subcommittee), where designated representatives from police, education and health participate in the active provision of services to the child or young person concerned.

Providing safe accommodation throughout periods of 'going missing'

We have noted that it is not until a young person can begin to feel safe and confident that practitioners are working in their best interest that they may begin to disclose details of the trafficking experiences they have been through. Practitioners who had experience of working with trafficked young people to achieve this aim recognised that there might be repeat episodes of the young person going missing while they 'tested' out the home, or that traffickers might abduct or entice the young person away from the placement. It was acknowledged that a young person may go missing for some time, but experience suggested that they may well return, particularly if they know there is a 'safe place' and a 'safe relationship' to return to. One practitioner noted how many young people do return after going missing, even sometimes after a year:

> They have come back . . . They feel safe there . . . We have had young people . . . who have gone missing quite close to arrival, so before we've had very much information on them at all, and have come back down

the line, like several months later, some even a year or so later. There's not a lot of those, there have been a handful of them but enough . . .

(Interview 13)

In another example of this happening, the young person returned and brought another vulnerable young person with her: 'She was placed in emergency accommodation here but went missing before any assessment could be undertaken . . . and returned with another Chinese young female who was not known to us' (CS004). This led to a recognition that practical support, such as the provision of leaflets and addresses or ensuring that contact numbers are recorded on mobile phones, helped the young person to feel that they were kept in mind: 'and they have fed back that having a place to come back to, knowing where that is, is what has allowed them to do that. Which again is some of our thought process behind the leaflet . . .' (Interview 13). In some situations, contact could be maintained through telephone conversations:

> For the first six weeks that the young person went missing, a police officer from the Sexual Exploitation Unit had weekly telephone contact with the young person who outlined that she was safe at that time. The police officer arranged to meet with the young person on several occasions but the young person failed to show, young person's phone was turned off and contact could not be made.
>
> (CS030)

The practitioners above are illustrating that the process of settling into the place of safety may take a while, and that it is helpful for the young person to feel that they are being kept in mind, even if they go missing. This 'being kept in mind' was a significant factor in securing the well-being of the young person during the process of settling into the UK.

Conclusion

This chapter has explored the use of specialist and dedicated services that need to be targeted towards trafficked children and young people. This does not imply that the trafficked child is inherently 'different' from other children and young people. As argued in chapter 6, universal mainstream services have a responsibility to make their services accessible to all children and young people. However, this chapter notes that some of the experiences of the trafficked child or young person can precipitate needs and behaviours that require specialist intervention. To summarise, this means meeting the young person from the outset with a child-centred rather than an immigration approach to intervention, ensuring that an age assessment or other intrusive interventions do not take place at the expense of the young person's safety or well-being. It means providing a trained and supported 'key worker' who can oversee support throughout the transitions taking place in the child's life. Each agency supporting the trafficked child needs to recognise the importance of training and supporting their own staff to be able to engage with the work appropriately. In addition, specialist, trained and supported foster or residential carers are needed at the very point of the young person's entry to the UK and in the immediate aftermath to secure safety through a 'front loading' approach to intervention. With 24-hour support from police and child care agencies, these placements could provide safe accommodation for the young person, both at the point of arrival into the country and through longer term provision, enabling them to settle and engage with mainstream activities, such as attending school and youth and health services. Episodes of 'going missing' need to be understood in the context of previous abuse and of abduction and with an awareness of the effect of exploitation that may, through default, have resulted in the young person's misguided attachment to those who have abused them. Enabling the young person to understand the impact of this abuse and to begin to develop self-determined steps to maintain their own safety and well-being will take time and, it is argued, is best achieved through modelling 'good' relationships with a carer and key worker.

We move now to look at two other specialist services that, we argue, are essential to helping a trafficked young person make the transition from 'victim' to active agent in the development of their long-term safety.

8 Specialist interpreters and mental health providers

We have noted in chapter 7 that specialist services are needed at the trafficked young person's point of arrival to the UK. These include both the allocation of a trained and supported key worker and a place of safety. In this chapter we explore findings from our research that suggested the need for two other specialist services: a trained and supported interpreter service and appropriate mental health interventions. We conclude by arguing that, while essential, none of these services can function if they are working in isolation from each other. We see how a multi-agency framework can support practitioners in engaging with and supporting the young person while sharing information that is needed to secure a coherent, active child protection plan and to disrupt, and indeed finally prosecute abusers.

The use of interpreters: complexities emerging in practice

Before specifically addressing the issues that emerged from our research about the need for trained and specialist interpreters, it is helpful to address the significance, raised by many practitioners, of the relationship between language and the young person's experience of abuse. The 'process' of being trafficked within and between different countries as described in chapter 4 can often prevent the young person from communicating with anyone other than their traffickers. The young person, who will probably only communicate in the language of their country of origin, will either not be in one place for long enough to learn the basics of a new language, or will be prevented from meeting others who might advise them. On the one hand, language can be used as a tool to connect the child to those who are abusing them:

> She apparently meets two people at the airport who are speaking her language and then goes to stay with them for two weeks . . . we know that this set-up isn't right. People who are strangers . . . they approach

them and these people automatically take them in . . . They could be a risk of any sort.

(Interview 23)

On the other hand, language can be used to isolate them from seeking help outside their communities. Indeed, although it might be assumed that a shared language is a source of support, for many young people it was the shared language that made them more vulnerable to being manipulated and abused. As noted in chapter 5, an interviewee noted: 'And again, the people that are trafficking them know that they're most likely to trust someone who speaks their own language' (Interview 14). It cannot therefore be assumed that the 'shared' community is actually the 'safe' community. Assessments about where the best support will be found need to be based on an assessment of the ability of the adult or the community to care for the child as opposed to being able to speak the same language. If the potential carers do speak the same language as the young person this may well help them in the process of settling and engaging, but practitioners noted the need for caution against allowing the same language to take precedence over other concerns.

If language differences do exist between the young person, their carer and/or the key work practitioner, an interpreter may be needed. This, of course, leads to important questions about the selection, training and support of the interpreters who will be used to engage with the young person solely because they can communicate in the same language. Interpreters will need to be aware of the possibility of language being used as a means of control and manipulation and be mindful of the impact that this might have on engaging with the young person and on the information the young person may feel confident enough to give them.

The role of the interpreter and the specific issues identified by practitioners about managing the complexities in this role are addressed below.

The engagement and use of interpreters

There were some differences between the account which we got via the language line and the subsequent interviews which she gave . . . The number of interpreters was very limited, the number of these specialist language interpreters is fairly limited.

(Interview 30)

The facts can be passed on, but you cannot always pass the emotions, no matter how good you are as an interpreter.

(CS015)

The two quotes above indicate some of the complexities that emerge when interpreters are used to support communication between practitioners and young people who have been trafficked. It may be hard to locate a trained and appropriate interpreter; the extent of emotional harm caused to the young person may go undetected, 'lost in translation'; and the interpreter may be poorly equipped to understand or communicate the nature of the abuse as experienced by the young person.

The dynamics between the young person, the practitioner and the interpreter

Noting the above, it was recognised that while the use of an interpreter for a trafficked young person may place specific pressures on both, there might be particular dynamics to be mindful of in the process taking place between all the parties involved, including those outside the immediate relationship between the young person and their interpreter. One of these is in managing the length of time that is taken during the translation process: 'You've got a question, you've got the interpreter translating it, you've got the answer in the foreign language, you've got the interpreter translating it back . . . it's like watching paint dry' (CS015). Being sensitive to the dynamics that can occur between the interpreter, the young person and the other practitioners involved also meant being aware of cultural issues that might come into play. For example, a respondent noted:

> we have to look at it through the victim's cultural values . . . In some cultures women are regarded as second rate. So while we naturally assume female victim, female officer, female interviewer, in actual fact, some cases they'll think: 'I'm getting a second rate service here – they don't believe me. Why aren't I getting a man to deal with me?'
>
> (CS015)

In addition, the interpreter may, in ways unknown to the practitioners, offend the young person through the use of a particular word or phrase. All of these possible scenarios need to be taken into account and, wherever possible, the young person should be consulted about the timing, location and content of interviews, their views being taken into consideration.

The extended role of the interpreter

> The people to use are the interpreters. They can tell you so much about the background, the culture of the place. You've really got to tap into them, A good interpreter is key . . .
>
> (Interview 17)

If the interpreter is able to create a feeling of safety and trust, they by default become part of a process of 'bearing witness' to what has happened to the young person (Hynes 2003). This may assist the young person's recovery, giving them a feeling of being believed, with credibility given to their account of events. For example, during a looked-after child review interview, a social worker noted:

> she attended this review and contributed to discussions via the interpreter. She cried quite a lot during the review . . . It was explained that the assessment must be completed as social services have a duty to care . . . During the review she raised [the issue] that she wanted to leave the placement.
>
> (CS028)

The interpreter needed to be able to witness and withstand the young person's distress. While allowing the young person to be upset, the challenge was also to convey how important it was that the review continued, without undermining the impact it was having on her. The interpreter needed to be skilled enough to be able to work within this context, being part of managing the young person's distress and emotional state while also responding to the practitioner's need to continue with the interview.

The need for training for 'specialist' interpreters to work with trafficked young people

As noted, it was evident from our research that it was important for interventions to be supported by interpreters who had been trained to understand the implications of working with young people who had been trafficked. A sensitive interpreter was required at many levels, even at times for something as basic as recording the child or young person's name.

> I mean how can . . . their names don't actually translate . . . if the young person couldn't read and write in their own language the way the name would be written would be the name that the interpreter wrote. When we had the first planning meeting we'd ask the child to say how they thought their name was spelt, they'd work it out with their interpreter, then we would agree a spelling.
>
> (Interview 6)

The interpreter may need to be prepared to be upset, disbelieving or confused by some of the details disclosed by the young person. They will also need to be aware that they themselves may be approached to work for traffickers or may be threatened by traffickers and those who work with them. Indeed, the young person may have been instructed by traffickers not to answer any questions at all and to avoid contact with interpreters. This means the interpreter needs to be able to acknowledge potential distrust and be able to work with distressed behaviour while interpreting and translating. They will need to be mindful to convey empathy and encouragement during the interview, and recognise the importance of creating an atmosphere of support and belief, rather than one where the young person feels interrogated or disbelieved.

To undertake this task, it was noted that the interpreter will need to be able to manage fear and distrust that may be felt by the young person if they are faced with an interpreter from the same community or of the same cultural or racial origin as the people who trafficked them. These additional pressures mean that interpreters themselves may need support in managing the feelings evoked when listening to and recounting stories of trauma and abuse.

The potential harm caused by using untrained interpreters

It was noted that damage could be caused if the interpreter was not prepared for the possibilities of difficult details emerging throughout the course of an interview. For example, a social work key worker recounted an experience with a Chinese young woman who had been trafficked into the country and then held in a brothel and raped. Following identification, the worker and an interpreter accompanied the young woman to a doctor as she had a pain in her arm. She noted how the interpreter, who was not adequately trained to manage complex cases, failed to communicate appropriately and disrupted the developing trust that the key worker felt she was building with the child:

> [the doctor] found it was a contraceptive implant . . . I'm still duty bound to tell her what it is, because it's her option as to whether she wants it left in or out because it's hurting her . . . I said (to the interpreter), 'Look, this is quite difficult to explain so rather than interpreting exactly what I say to you, if you can tell her that, what we believe is, she's got a contraceptive implant, and that if we take it out, were she to have sex with anyone she may get pregnant, but that's a decision down to her. Can you interpret for me?' She said yes. So she interpreted it and then turned back to me and said she had said I've told her that what's in her arm is one of those things that married couples use to stop getting pregnant.

(CS011)

The interpreter had explained the situation to the young woman in a way that she felt would be accessible and understandable to the child. The key worker, however, went on to express some concerns. She was worried that the interpreter's ability to explain what the implant was, why it might have been administered and how it related to the young woman's experiences of abuse was limited, closing down the conversation through the reference to marriage and family life. She did not feel confident that the young woman understood the reason for the implant, its removal or other forms of contraception that might be available to her if needed. The key worker had not wanted to prolong the time in the doctor's surgery and could see that the young woman was both embarrassed and tired by the appointment. As the booking and payment of interpreters was established on an hourly basis and funds for using interpreters were limited, she was concerned that there was not enough time in this session to take the point further and that in order to raise the topic again she might have to draw on another interpreter, something she did not want to do because it would mean that the young woman would have to have her circumstances exposed to yet another adult.

In a different case, the social work key worker voiced concern that an untrained interpreter might not only change the meaning of the conversation, but might actually fail to interpret some content they were uncomfortable with, or shocked by. Sometimes, the extent of abuse and distress portrayed by the young person was difficult for the interpreter to manage:

> Looking at the . . . experience of the interpreters in dealing with these young people because the interpreter that we had . . . was obviously shocked by what she was hearing . . . That was a joint interview I did with a police officer and both of us had the same anxieties about what was being interpreted . . . I think it's around developing a specialist interpreter.
>
> (Interview 9)

In contrast to the concern that there might be a disjuncture between the experience of the interpreter and that of the child, there was the concern that the interpreter might over-identify with the child, possibly creating inappropriate relationships that blurred the boundary between the role of interpreter and the role of friend. It was noted that there were ample opportunities for the interpreter and the child to become attached as a result of sharing personal information. If an interpreter is allocated to a particular case, or is called back to interpret for a child more than once, it is possible that the beginnings of a relationship will become established. This is very likely where the interpreter is working with sensitive material and is empathising with the child, accommodating the different moods and feelings that emerge over the course of an interview. It is these dynamics that place a particular strain on interpreters and mean that training in the nature of trafficking and the policies and procedures in place to work with trafficking of young people is essential.

The advantages of using a trained interpreter

The following case gives some insight into the pressures facing interpreters, who need to gain the young person's trust while maintaining clear boundaries around their role and purpose. In this case, it was noted that the advantage of employing a trained and supported interpreter was evident and that their role was essential to securing a prosecution after the young person had pursued charges against an alleged trafficker.

This young woman had turned up at a police station after escaping from a nightclub. She said that she had been trafficked into the country, sold more than three times, raped and used for sex. The interpreter noted their own feelings of conflict as they built a relationship with the young woman, observing how difficult it was to manage the delicate boundary between being an interpreter and becoming a friend. The interpreter notes:

> It took time to warm up to her and it took her time to warm up to me. There's no way she's going to say everything to me within the first minute she sees me because I'm not there to make friendship with her. I'm there in a professional role as an interpreter and I basically convey from one side to another what was being said. So it did take time for us to establish that close sort of, I wouldn't say friendship, but yes she felt . . . though I'm almost twice her age . . . perhaps trust as well and get over shock from what she had been in the last three or four months before she met me. But I think we built through that period of time a very strong bond and she felt very comfortable, very comfortable and confident telling me . . . I think because, being from that country myself, you sort of know how perhaps to approach, slowly and gently and not in a horrible way and she sort of gave in.
>
> (CS015c)

This interpreter managed the boundary between interpreter and friend well, securing the positive relationship and supporting the young woman to disclose difficult information about her circumstances. A different practitioner working on the same case noted:

> I think its fair to say that had it not been for the second interpreter , we

wouldn't have had a job . . . she did an outstanding effort on this young girl, from befriending her, to being able to relate to her . . .

(CSO15b)

These quotations show the delicate balance that the interpreter needs to maintain between creating a feeling of trust with the young person while retaining a professional relationship. The role that this particular interpreter played was not only important to the young woman concerned, but also to the other practitioners involved in the case and to the prosecution. There was evidence that through the course of their work the interpreter might identify 'intelligence' that could later be used in a case against a perpetrator: 'We had a phone call from the barrister in London who'd got a case which was linked with our name; the only reason he knew was because we had used the same translator who noticed the link' (CS015b). Those who worked on this particular case and were interviewed for the research all felt that the case might not have moved to prosecution without the relationship this young woman was able to build with the interpreter:

> The times we had to use an independent interpreter for court and things like that and you got somebody else in, you could see the shutters went up on the young girl and she was like 'No, I want my interpreter'.
>
> (CS015b)

In summary, practitioners suggest that there is a need for specialist interpreters who have been trained in interviewing techniques with damaged and difficult young people. The interpreters used for these cases need to be aware of child protection legislation and policies and procedures, and be mindful of the boundary they will have to maintain between being a confidant, on the one hand, and a professional interpreter, on the other. In addition, the interpreter will need to be aware that the young person they are interpreting for might, at some point, be providing intelligence that can be used as evidence in court. The interpreter may need help in managing both the bond and the threat that their own nationality might present to the young person, and feel confident in managing this throughout the process of interpreting. Finally, they need to understand and manage the risks that might be presented to them if they were to be identified by traffickers. They may be targeted because they are supporting police-led investigations. These pressures mean that training and support structures need to be in place for interpreters who specialise in work with trafficked young people.

We move now to looking at the second service identified in this chapter as being an essential specialist service for trafficked young people: the provision of specialist and supported mental health workers.

Mental health services for trafficked young people

> [She] states she can't talk about what she has been through with any-one. She can't even talk about it to her best friend because she doesn't want to remember what happened to her . . .
>
> (CS003)

In chapter 6 we looked at some of the generic issues raised for health services when identifying and caring for trafficked young people. We noted the important role that all health services can play, particularly those located in sexual health services, in accident and emergency and as nurses in schools. Here, we go into a little more detail about the need for specialist and trained child and adolescent mental health services (CAMHS). This is prompted by the range of severe mental health issues presented by the young people who had been trafficked. It was widely recognised that the impact of trauma and abuse had significant consequences for their mental health, and that these consequences need particular attention.

Previous chapters have already identified the extreme trauma, distress and accumulated loss many young people have experienced before leaving their country of origin or during their journeys (Chase *et al.* 2008: 2). While the research by Chase *et al.* reveals gaps in terms of appropriate mental health services, it also highlights the need for developing an appropriate language for mental health that is less stigmatised and better understood by young people across a range of cultures (2008: 3). This argument is well developed by Coleman (2011) in relation to mental health services for adolescents overall. In terms of meeting the needs of refugee, unaccompanied asylum-seeking or trafficked young people, both Chase *et al.* (2008) and Kohli and Mitchell (2007) note that the young person's behaviour needs to be understood in context. For example, the more vulnerable the young person is, the more likely they are to be implicated in offences orchestrated by the traffickers. It was not uncommon for trafficked young people to be encouraged to recruit others into exploitative situations.

This young woman presented a very difficult case because she was suffering from a range of different mental health problems:

> given to us as a trafficking case . . . unclear if girl actually trafficked into the UK for exploitation or whether she came to live with an aunt after her caregivers in Africa had deceased. Her engagement in sexual exploitation was both putting herself at risk as well as grooming other girls, may be a consequence of personal trauma suffered in Africa and sexual exploitation/child prostitution in the UK. Her mental health is of great concern as she suffers from mood swings, displays

violent behaviour, self harms and has been suicidal on a number of occasions.

(CS029)

If the young person has experienced being trafficked, exploited and abused, as well as being displaced from 'home', their needs may be overwhelming – overwhelming both for themselves and others they are in contact with. As noted in chapter 1, this need not mean that aspects of recovery are impossible. Practitioners did not argue for a separate, specialist mental health intervention for trafficked young people. Instead, they argued that CAMHS workers should be provided with additional training to extend their capacity to identify cases and engage with the issues presented. This should enable them to recognise the indicators, be tolerant of the time taken by a young person to disclose, and know when and how to work with other agencies, such as police, child protection workers and local authority carers.

Developing 'time aware' mental health services

Most of all, training for mental health work in touch with trafficked young people would encourage workers to be prepared to believe and address the extent of harm experienced by the young person, recognising the length of time that it might take before disclosure, engagement and recovery take place. For example, a residential worker talked of the withdrawn state of a young man from abroad:

> [He had been] kidnapped with mother and sister and locked in a room in a house for a long period of time. They had little food or water. His sister was raped repeatedly, became ill and died, but the body remained in the room with him and his mum for a long period of time. Unclear what happened to mother. When escaped from room, a man offered to get him to the UK.
>
> (CS018)

The young man in this case was referred to CAMHS for support. He needed intensive contact with the CAMHS worker over a long period of time before he was able to discuss the impact his experiences had had on him.

Similarly, a number of cases of self-harm and attempted suicide were reported:

> She reported suffering from headaches which do not ease. There are concerns about her emotional well-being, not sleeping, nightmares,

suicidal thoughts and self-harm. She has previously planned to kill herself by drinking bleach in initial health assessment.

(CS001)

Another young woman was noted to have:

mood swings, displays violent behaviour, allegedly tried to kill another young person, and self-harms. A lot of assessments were made, three interventions at three different adolescent psychiatric departments but no mental health diagnosis made . . . A referral to CAMHs was suggested as well as a behavioural programme in a residential or secure unit . . .

(CS029)

And a young man who was trafficked for sexual exploitation:

has on several occasions attempted to swallow tacks, pieces of broken glass and CDs. He has stated that he has at times thought of throwing himself off a bridge over a motorway and has indicated that he does not think he will be alive in two years' time.

(CS031)

These cases illustrate the range of pressures experienced by some of the young people who had been trafficked and suggest that trained and supported mental health workers are needed to address the issues presented. As noted above, this relies on the mental health practitioner both being open to identifying a young person's previous trafficking trajectory and working creatively with any issues that might emerge.

Managing disclosure and supporting longer term interventions

As explored in earlier chapters, it is evident that few trafficked young people will immediately disclose information about the abuse they have experienced. Indeed, many employ sophisticated ways to avoid talking about the impact of the abuse on their lives:

Right at the moment she doesn't want to talk to anyone, she's keeping it very private. But you know it's a door that should never be closed because at one point she might actually say 'What happened to me was wrong and I don't want it to happen to any other children, therefore I would like to talk.'

(CS011)

Many young people did appear, at face value, to manage on their own, rejecting any support in addressing the impact of abuse. This was particularly common for young men, as can be seen by practitioners' comments on two separate cases: 'Emotionally well balanced and able to take care of himself . . . suppressing his emotions' (CS002); and 'He had regularly said that he was not going to talk' (CS023). Mental health workers played an important role in supporting the young person through the process of disclosure and helping them to manage the feelings that were associated with this disclosure. For this service to access and engage trafficked children, particular methods of intervention are needed. For example, in one locality there was a specific project targeted at supporting young people's well-being. It was a generic project targeted at providing CAMHS services for vulnerable and marginalised young people. Following a health assessment, the project tailored specific work for the young people by linking CAMHS workers with other youth work and child protection staff. Employing a child psychologist, a counsellor and an administrator, the project used different mechanisms to engage with the young people and was able to focus on identifying signs of trafficking.

> It's through the health assessment . . . what's called the well-being project . . . a CAMHS project . . . Obviously that's a project and has time-limited funding, so we don't know what's happening after that . . . When we see a young person we do a full physical examination, looking for evidence . . . any concern they have we look at.
>
> (Interview 9)

The advantage of developing close links between CAMHS workers and other professions tasked to support vulnerable young people is that holistic support can be provided. This was particularly important in linking young people into services that could help them with drug-related problems. For example, this young woman from the UK:

> [She is a] severely depressed, vulnerable individual who is sexually exploited, has drug issues and is at risk of self-harm through overdosing and is risk to herself and other young people . . . [She] needs [a] psychological and psychiatric assessment to determine the level of damage . . .
>
> (CS022)

This example of a practice setting illustrates the importance of CAMHS being child centred and aware of the specific dynamics created both through adolescence and through experiences of trafficking. It also illustrates the importance of multi-agency working, with practitioners knowing who to approach in related child care service providers and when and why to share information. We turn now to look at this in more detail.

Multi-agency working

Chapters 4 to 7 gave an insight into some of the pressures facing both the trafficked young people and their practitioners. Examples of good and not so good practice have been suggested, with the overriding themes that identification and engagement are essential components in offering long-term support to the trafficked child and that training and support are needed for staff once the work develops with the child. The experience of being trafficked is isolating. If the services that support the trafficked child are also isolated from each other, failing to support each other's efforts to enable the young person to have access to a settled home, to health, education and employment, the isolation becomes embedded and permanent. If keeping the child or young person safe means that agencies are to share information effectively, and establish joint interventions with individual cases, they must establish genuine and effective multi-agency work.

Developing effective protocols to guide multi-agency work

While there were many examples of cooperation, there was a concern that the good intention of agencies to work together could be hampered by staff feeling overburdened. There was a worry that developing multi-agency work with trafficked young people could place an unwelcome strain on already stretched resources. 'All services suffer from a lack of staff at the moment but in itself that makes working together extremely difficult' (Interview 27). Despite these pressures, it was felt important for individual agencies to provide a protocol for its staff, outlining what their service can offer to keep the young person safe. Sometimes these were best developed by drawing on the experience of practice. 'We've developed protocols from the way we work . . . because it's very important that we can define what we do, so we're more open and people look at what we do for us to improve' (Interview 4).

The local protocol was helpful when trying to follow through joint work with other agencies: 'and we may use some of those protocols in terms of getting action from others' (Interview 12). However, it was noted that developing an effective protocol took time and resources, and that its creation could become 'yet another job to be done' if it was not supported properly. For example, a health worker acknowledged that the development of a protocol might be a task for the future, but that his service was already stretched:

I am sure there is one in social services, but we don't have one in health as far as I know, specifically because, as I say, most of the time they don't get to my service . . . I suppose it's a gap. It is one of those things where it is on a never-ending list of things that you have got to do . . . There is only one of me and the number of children and the changes of policies are never-ending . . . I think we are reviewing at least 70 young people at any one time.

(Interview 2)

Invariably, policy makers would suggest that protocols were effective tools for making the case for the need for resources for work with trafficked children. In short, if there was a document saying collaboration was needed, giving guidance about how and when agencies should play the different roles, it was easier to argue for resources to make the work happen. However, some practitioners were cautious, considering that they were almost overburdened by protocols and directives. One noted that a protocol is only as effective as its implementation, and that if staff are overburdened they may overlook the requirements for joint work: 'got a runaways protocol . . . the difficulty we're finding at the moment is trying to get agencies committed to it' (Interview 19). Another practitioner noted difficulty in ensuring the involvement of all agencies, finding that time was spent in ensuring that law enforcement as well as the appropriate child protection teams were working together.

I mean I just do think that the UKBA needs to make far, far, far better links with the whole multi-agency group . . . we've got to make good relationships with CPS [Crown Prosecution Service]. And it's borough police that we're doing this work with, not the child abuse investigation teams.

(Interview 10)

It is clear that the aim of keeping the young person safe cannot be achieved without the full participation of the range of child protection and law enforcement agencies. Local protocols which guide practice are needed but are ineffective without the resources available to support the staff involved. If these resources are not in place, practitioners may feel daunted by the range of needs presented by the trafficked young person, by the dangers faced from organised crime, and by their potential failure to prevent harm. Although failing to identify and engage with cases cannot be condoned, the pressures facing staff need to be understood and addressed.

Multi-agency working: benefits of working together to keep the young person safe

Despite the difficulties that were identified in working together, it was recognised that close collaboration between different agencies was essential for ensuring trafficked young people were kept safe and that their needs were met. For example, one practitioner noted how the assessment of a young person's needs was improved when child protection worked alongside immigration services. Referring to a multi-agency team based at the airport where child protection staff from the local safeguarding board can work alongside UK Border Agency staff, the practitioner observed that this dedicated team work was able to:

> make better assessments at the beginning so that you can have a safeguarding response, we've got that in place now . . . the case is both child protection and immigration case. The two areas of work have to be developed together.
>
> (Interview 5)

Another individual stressed that multi-agency work helps each professional to define and work to their own criteria and skills:

> Working together with other professionals – the more that happens the better it is for everyone . . . That frees us to support the young person . . . it allows each professional to fulfil their specific role as best as possible . . . No one agency can do it on their own . . . collaborating and working together but also keeping their roles to an extent as well.
>
> (Interview 13)

Some felt that good multi-agency work was best supported by guidance documents and local protocols, with a checklist to monitor the work undertaken by different agencies. However, as mentioned above, others were aware that while protocols were useful, good multi-agency work was best developed through experience. It was noted that 'working together' builds a team spirit which helps different agencies understand each other better: 'The relationship between children's services and immigration is improving as well . . . a few years ago you wouldn't have got them sitting in the same room' (CS010). Another interviewee commented:

> Because of the numbers we have here . . . and the agencies we work with . . . we're quite established in setting up the networks that we have here to work with . . . schools, health workers, social workers and the

police . . . [We] can get them referred to CAMHS . . . getting extra support in terms of foster placements – if the carers need extra support we can put that in place.

(Interview 12)

This experience meant a sharing of policy and practice, resulting in a shared responsibility for the young person, with the result that there was less scope for the young person to be 'forgotten' during periods of going missing. As noted by a police officer working on a case of a young person trafficked for sexual exploitation: 'You are like a mechanism where each one of you is accountable to each other. You're bringing in different expertise' (Interview 10). Another pointed out: 'One of the obstacles is having limited information . . . no concrete information that gives us anything to investigate, then it sort of goes dead . . . they may go missing down the line' (Interview 13). When a range of workers are focused on 'holding the young person in mind' (see chapter 6), there is more possibility that intelligence about their whereabouts and wellbeing is identified. It was seen as important that this varied expertise is understood and respected:

With the best will in the world, social workers are social workers, police officers are police officers. While we try to dabble in each other's work, we know what we want and others know what they want. They wouldn't have gone out with an evidential head on. You know, they just want to know where this baby's come from, whereas I want to know how to get the information into court to bolster my prosecution against this woman.

(CS010)

Sharing information between agencies working together

Being able to share information, and understand the roles and requirements of different agencies is essential when maintaining a focus on keeping the young person safe. One model which shows how to achieve this 'keeping the young person in mind' is the practice established by many local authorities for safeguarding sexually exploited children and young people. This model consists of three components:

• A multi-agency subgroup of the Safeguarding Board following a protocol that informs staff in the borough of procedures they should follow and agencies they should refer to in potential and confirmed cases of trafficking.

- Allocation of a lead professional from each service (youth work, CAMHS, sexual health, education, including individual schools, drug and alcohol services, police, CPS, youth offending team) to attend the Safeguarding Board subgroup meetings. Depending on the size and role of the service involved, it may need to develop its own protocol (in line with the Local Safeguarding Board's protocol) to guide the practitioners on how to respond.
- A specialist and trained youth work service that can act as a resource for ongoing contact work with the young people. Ideally, it includes staff employed to provide outreach and therapeutic services.

Research and evaluation in the field has demonstrated that this model works effectively through multi-agency work (Scott and Skidmore 2006). Practitioners from one site interviewed for our research referred to this model as one that was effective, noting that the development of the Multi-Agency Public Protection Arrangements (MAPPA) also helps to formalise the organisation of joint work through multi-agency partnerships. MAPPA is the name for arrangements between 'responsible authorities' such as police, probation and prison authorities who are tasked with the management of registered sex offenders, violent and other types of sexual offenders, and offenders who pose a serious risk of harm to the public. Public Protection Units (PPUs) are the local forums where such multi-agency work takes place. As noted by a practitioner:

> We've got our own dedicated police officer for sexual exploitation . . . For every young person identified there's at least an initial assessment done by a social worker, the strategy meeting . . . obviously you've got the police there . . . chaired by the detective inspector from the PPU . . . we've got a drugs worker as well and we work closely with the youth work part of the service.
>
> (Interview 18)

It was through these formal structures that practitioners gained the knowledge and confidence of how and when to share information, supporting each other in the efforts to keep the young person safe, prevent episodes of going missing and gathering intelligence that could be used as evidence against abuser(s). The research noted, however, that even when structures were in place, practitioners might approach the problems faced by trafficked young people from very different perspectives. These needed identifying and working with to prevent agencies being 'split' from each other and to secure genuinely shared roles in delivering care plans.

Reconciling difference: creating a shared focus on keeping the trafficked child safe

It was evident that one of the key components of good practice in working together was the capacity for each agency to understand and respect the different roles they play in safeguarding trafficked young people.

For example, the police and the Crown Prosecution Service are tasked with gathering intelligence about the perpetrators of the crime, and with considering the viability of taking a case through court, meaning that they will look at a case through a particular lens, with a focus on using the range of agencies necessary for gathering intelligence. 'If you carry out an examination and you find semen inside her then yes, you can prosecute. I have prosecuted on that basis before, but someone's got to think to organise the medical examination' (Interview 30). The practitioner making the medical examination may not have had the gathering of evidence for a prosecution in mind, focusing more on the medical well-being of the young person as their primary aim.

The police here noted that although they were specifically looking for intelligence that could be used as evidence, they recognised that they themselves might not be the best agency to gather this intelligence. They were aware that during the course of work with a youth worker, a social worker or an education practitioner, a young person might give information that could be used as evidence against a perpetrator. An example was given where a young person was 'able to describe the organised abuse' to their key worker, but when interviewed by police 'they have not been able to recognise and recall any street names, addresses or phone numbers or even any accurate names and descriptions that might lead the police to a prosecution' (CS003).

While this focus on 'intelligence' may sound clinical, it is an essential component in securing prosecutions and furthering the safety of the young person. While the need for practitioners to work together to gather intelligence is established, it is recognised that different agencies will have different roles in supporting the young person's welfare.

The need for training in multi-agency work: implementing protocols

The issues raised above argue that each local agency should have a protocol that clarifies its role and resource allocation to trafficked children and young people. Whether the protocol is adapted from one that has been used by another geographical area, or generated from an agency's own local practice, its existence can provide practitioners with a 'tool' to use when developing a momentum for initiating multi-agency provision.

However, as noted, the existence of a protocol is not enough. Training is needed to bring staff together within and between agencies to address how they each identify and support trafficked young people. It was proposed that each agency have a lead practitioner whose brief was to lead the development of training and practice in this area: 'what the protocols are for and to develop awareness in the first place . . . then we need some training, we need to have lead professionals in agencies who know more than the rest about it' (Interview 19).

A central component of staff training was the need for staff from different agencies to train and work together, to break down barriers that might be developed because of a perceived 'hierarchy' of skills, knowledge and experience. While it was recognised that different professionals had different tasks, roles and responsibilities, these should not privilege one profession over another: 'Sometimes the person who has seen the child protection issue is a housing official. They've got it right, they've reported it but no notice is taken of it, because of the source it came from' (CS020).

Indeed, casework showed how important joint work and information sharing was between some universal service providers, such as housing, which might not immediately be considered to play an important role in safeguarding trafficked children and young people:

> so there's a team manager and a couple of housing officers all of whom have had dealings with this woman . . . They knew the woman's teenage child was no longer in the country, so she'd lost entitlement to housing, or she went further down the list, so they evicted her from the accommodation she had. As a result of that she went to Nigeria to get the baby . . . The arrest was planned, we got social services with us because clearly there was going to be a baby and a teenager there . . . When we went in the girl really worried me . . . she just lay there on the bed looking at us . . . she was very withdrawn . . . We worked together, at the legal strategy meeting we decided we were going to work together . . . That case was a really good example of working together . . . everyone was quite open with each other and I think everyone acted in the best interest of that baby.
>
> (CS010)

These illustrations from practice show that if practitioners from various agencies are provided with opportunities to both train and work together, their interventions with the young people model a 'joined up' experience. In essence, this means that rather than give the young person the message that agencies are in conflict with each other, they portray collaboration and support for each other. This makes it more difficult for a young person to

split one agency from the other or to experience a disjuncture between interventions. While this 'joined up' approach may be an ideal to work towards
as opposed to a reality in everyday practice, it should not be discarded as
an aim. As the key worker approach gives a model of a good relationship,
so too does effective multi-agency work give a model of shared practice: a
model that will equip the young person to move into adulthood asking for
and expecting clarity in roles, responsibilities and boundaries in their future
negotiations.

Conclusion

The trafficked young person and their practitioners need access to specialist
interpreters who have been trained to understand the child protection issues
presented in trafficking cases, and trained in methods of engaging with difficult and damaged young people. This training needs to include awareness of
the impact of language and its importance to an abused and trafficked young
person, and appreciation of the boundaries between acting as a professional
and as a friend.

This chapter has also argued that the young person needs support with
mental health provision so that they can begin to manage the implications
of the specific nature of the abuse they have experienced. Sustained and
consistent support may be needed over time to allow for disclosure. With
support, the young person may gradually be able to take more control over
their circumstances, gain a better understanding of their own mental health
needs and work with practitioners to address them.

In summary, this chapter has argued that multi-agency work helps both
to share knowledge and experience and to mitigate feelings of isolation for
practitioners and the young people they support. A number of cases illustrated the need for all universal service providers to be tasked with responsibility for identifying and working with trafficked young people, and to be
given training to meet those tasks. If this training is shared between professions, practitioners can better understand the boundaries between the remits
of the services they provide and ways of collaborating to maximise the benefit for the young person. Throughout the chapter it has been argued that
while a protocol is helpful as a tool to clarify roles and to campaign internally for resources within a particular agency, it is not enough on its own.
Experience of joint work brings a genuine sharing of practice and expertise.
Through evaluation and sharing of experience of multi-agency work, the
overall service for the trafficked young person can be improved.

9 Conclusions

This chapter summarises the main themes that have emerged throughout the process of undertaking this research, considering methods of data collection and issues arising from data analysis. It then moves to look at some of the longer term implications of the work, suggesting ways forward for developing better practice with trafficked young people.

Drawing on evidence from interviews and focus groups with child care practitioners and from case studies of trafficked young people, we have identified considerations to be addressed when undertaking research in this area. These include an appreciation of ethical considerations arising from interviewing practitioners who are working to pressurised timelines with full caseload commitments; the need to safeguard trafficked young people by upholding confidentiality; and the need to be mindful of the researchers' well-being, which can be challenged by 'living with' the collation, analysis and reporting of data exposing abuse and exploitation of young people.

Themes emerging from the research

This book has argued that trafficked young people need to be understood first and foremost as victims of child abuse. We clarify the contradictions in applying this approach to work with adolescents who may be exerting their agency in their move towards adulthood, but note throughout that the impact of the abuse and exploitation they have experienced must be understood and addressed by child protection policies and procedures. While the responsibility for this rests with all practitioners from all agencies working with young people, the Local Safeguarding Children Boards have, as lead child protection agencies, the central statutory duty for ensuring the protection of the young person.

We find that the processes by which young people are trafficked and the implications that remain for them are poorly understood by many practitioners, the complexities invariably being hidden behind a 'wall of silence' and a 'culture of disbelief'. We note that the key worker system, enabling trained and supported practitioners to manage sustained, 'good' relationships with the trafficked young person, can facilitate experience and understanding of a non-abusive relationship for the young person, which will, in turn, help them to separate from the trafficker(s). We draw on case study and interview data to illustrate both the difficulties in implementing this relationship based thinking and the advantages of so doing.

Our research findings show that all children's services have a role to play in identifying and supporting trafficked young people but that some dedicated, specialist provisions are needed, including a safe place at the point of arrival into the country, supported and trained carers to provide safe accommodation, trained interpreters to ensure that the young person is able to communicate in a safe environment, and experienced and specialist mental health workers to help the young person begin to address the harm they have experienced and to plan forward for recovery.

We explore three of these dominant findings in a little more detail below before moving to look at implications for future work.

Trafficking of young people is child abuse

One of the consistent themes emerging within the book is that despite the existing protocols, guidance and indeed recommendations from research for good practice that locate the trafficked young person as a 'victim' of child abuse, some practice interventions fail to engage from this premise. This happens for a number of complicated reasons. It may be that the practitioner has not received any training on the issues, an understandable possibility as no core compulsory training on trafficking of children and young people is required within child protection training for social work practitioners. Leading on from this, and perhaps even more particularly, it may be that practitioners have had little training or awareness of the particular dynamics occurring for young people during adolescence per se. Again, this may be understandable since core compulsory social work training does not insist on training in understanding adolescents or adolescence. Even the Munro (2011) review of child protection in the UK groups the needs of children and young people together, failing to require training and service development to separate out the particular safeguarding needs of abused adolescents as they make the transition to adulthood from the safeguarding needs of younger children abused within the home.

This is important because, while practitioners and agencies may intend to define the trafficked young person as a victim of child abuse, they struggle with the contradictions arising when many young people reject the 'victim' label, either consciously by aggressively exerting their agency by running away and/or rejecting support, or unconsciously by persistently colluding with the abuse they are experiencing. This collusion may result from coercion, manipulation or outright violence, but it is effective in portraying that there is nothing wrong or untoward in what has happened. This denial is often internalised by young people and believed by some practitioners whose intention it is to offer support. Further details of some of the processes involved in this denial are described by Pearce (forthcoming), who explores what she calls professional neglect through condoned consent.

Throughout the book we show that by locating the experiences of the young people as adolescents going through a stage of transition (moving from the status of child towards the status of adult), we gain a better understanding of the young person's developing agency, recognising their capacity to make decisions such as moving home, attending school or engaging in a sexual relationship. Mindful of this period of transition, we draw on case study and practitioner experience to note the unsettling impact of approaching the age of 18, when the young person's status in the country is reviewed and when they may be forcibly returned to somewhere identified as the 'home of origin'. The book has questioned the dominant perception of 'home', showing how many trafficked young people either do not know where the home of origin was, or have lived away for so long that 'home' is alien, or have traumatic memories of abuse, war, poverty and exploitation in their original 'home'. We have explored the implication of this for young people approaching adulthood, and note below that more work is needed in developing better awareness of both the source and destination countries of trafficked young people and in understanding what 'home' is and how it is constructed.

Most adolescents will be testing boundaries at this adolescent stage of their development, exploring their capacity within many other signifiers of the shift from child to adult (Coleman 2011). In this book we have argued that understanding this will help practitioners, and those in contact with a trafficked young person, to recognise why the young person may be trying to take matters into their own hands, making assertive comments about what they want to do and how they feel their actions are best supported. As observed throughout the book, the difference for the trafficked young person is that this transition is happening against a backdrop of abuse and exploitation. As opposed to enabling the young person to develop the skills and knowledge needed to manage a healthy transition, the trafficker(s) will, either forcibly or subtly, have engaged the young person in activities to meet the needs of the trafficker(s) rather than those of the young person.

This is child abuse. It is abuse that puts the young person into a 'victim' category, a category which, as noted, is at odds with 'self-determination' or 'personal agency'. We draw on a number of examples throughout the book to argue that traditional perceptions of child abuse, which have been influenced by child protection strategies targeting the protection of younger children rather than adolescents, do not include a sophisticated awareness either of how to recognise these subtle or violent forms of abuse or of how to respond to protect the young person and prosecute the abuser(s).

Although this is a dominant theme emerging from our research, it is important to note that this is not a new argument. Rees *et al.* (2010, 2011) talk about the long-term neglect of vulnerable adolescents in child protection interventions, and Jago *et al.* (2011) and Pearce (2009, 2011) refer to the long-standing denial by safeguarding boards and child protection agencies of the sexual exploitation of young people as a damaging form of child abuse.

What our work here suggests is that particular methods are required of engaging with young people who have been trafficked which recognise their need for boundaries and for secure relationships while also allowing them scope to develop autonomous decision making and self-determination. Training is needed to enable practitioners to engage with the complex dynamics of managing these processes while staying aware of the impact of previous and current abuse. That the basic generic, compulsory training in social work, teaching and mental health does not include this is indicative of the absence of thought and consideration given to safeguarding adolescents.

Trafficked young people are poorly understood

We have noted in the book that the definition of trafficking is sometimes confused, being used in different settings to apply to different young people. The trafficking of young people is often defined as smuggling, meaning that the exploitation experienced is overlooked. In addition, the trafficking of young people is often assumed to be for sexual exploitation, meaning that the lens for identification of abuse overlooks other forms of trafficking such as for domestic servitude, criminality or benefit fraud. The focus on sexual exploitation lends itself to encouraging a gender bias, meaning that sexually exploited young men are rarely identified.

We also identified how localities placed closer to airports are more likely to define trafficking as the movement of young people across international borders rather than as the movement of young people internally within the UK. These localities tend to gain a deeper understanding of the UK as a country of transit and destination and of the complex interrelationships between trafficking and different forms of exploitation, such as when a young person is used for both sex and drug trafficking, or for domestic servitude and sexual exploitation together. Localities further from airports or points of entry to the UK are less likely to define trafficking as involving movement across international borders and more likely to focus on 'internal' or 'domestic' trafficking of young people born in the UK for sexual exploitation.

While all forms of trafficking constitute abhorrent crimes against, and abuses of, the young person, our work suggests that further training is needed to ensure that practitioners are informed and able to identify the full range of methods and reasons for trafficking young people.

Putting the young person's needs first in multi-agency generic and specialist service provision

Our work has shown that it is evident that more should be done to understand the trafficking of young people as a child protection issue. Nowhere is this need so great as in the debate about age assessment and the process of putting the young person's needs before immigration concerns.

We have shown how, at the point of entry to the UK, young people are best protected by immediately being placed with trained and supported foster or residential care workers and by being allocated a statutory services key worker to oversee and hold responsibility for their care plan. We have noted the advantages of the allocation of a Guardian for the young person, but confirmed that this should not deflect attention from, or excuse moving it away from the need for statutory agencies to provide a 'key worker'. In addition, we have noted that if there are concerns that the age of the young person is unknown, this lack of knowledge should be understood as a result of the abuse rather than as the young person's own purposeful manipulation of authority. As such, age assessments should be integrated into a long-term care plan, rather than enacted at the point of arrival.

We have established that once the young person is engaged with their key worker in effecting a supported care plan, a number of service considerations follow. These may include using generic services such as school, sexual health services and accident and emergency health services, and more specialist services such as interpreter services and adolescent mental health services. The case materials and interviews reveal the complexities involved with putting some of these provisions into effect, but illustrate examples of good practice that can used for future learning.

We have explored how the full range of practitioners in schools, including school nurses, have an important role to play in helping the trafficked young person to integrate into the school, and have looked at the advantages and disadvantages of young people receiving their education within or outside the school environment. We noted how both educators and health care professionals play an important role in identifying trafficking in a young person's trajectory and, in particular, have looked at how information given through the process of disclosure may be collected as intelligence that may later be used as evidence in a prosecution against trafficker(s). Focusing on this, we have outlined the important relationship between both child care workers and police and other law enforcement agencies as they work together under multi-agency protocols to both protect the young person and prosecute abusers.

Advocating the advantages of multi-agency work, we have looked at some of the tensions that can occur between overstretched, and often increasingly under-resourced, service providers who are working within their own agency's parameters to demonstrate outcomes that are often unachievable with short-term funding. We acknowledge that this may have a negative impact on their capacity and ability to work in the multi-agency context. However, our research has shown that multi-agency working can safeguard the young person and result in prosecutions, but that this is only possible when practitioners feel resourced and supported to reach beyond their agency's borders. Work undertaken by Jago *et al.* (2011) shows how sexually exploited young people can be best protected through multi-agency work facilitated through co-located teams: practitioners, particularly police and child protection social workers, linked together through either virtual or physically connected teams. It may be that this model should be extended to working with trafficked young people.

We move now to draw on the three themes that have been outlined above to look at what an analysis of the research evidence suggests should happen next.

What needs to happen next?

Drawing on our data we identify two specific areas for development in the future. While we do not feel we are in a position to suggest how the development should take place, the research data clearly identify the need for further work in these three areas.

Training

As will have been seen, a number of training needs arise from the findings of this research. It is important to note that we do not see the provision of training as a 'sop', an answer to all problems or an excuse to shift attention away from the need for resources for service delivery. Instead we argue that it is essential that the core, generic training received by health, education, police and social work service providers includes both awareness of adolescence as a developmental stage for young people and the specific impact that abuse and exploitation can have on young people as they progress to adulthood.

This is particularly important for statutory child protection workers and we have described the intricate ways in which this can affect service delivery to safeguard adolescents. Without practitioners having this awareness and training on how to engage with and deliver services to exploited adolescents, young people will continue to be blamed for 'running away', challenging authority and for anti-social behaviour. While some young people are difficult and challenging, their behaviour needs to be understood in the context of abuse, and training in child protection both before and after qualifying needs to accommodate this. Of course, as argued throughout our book, this means locating older children and adolescents within the safeguarding agenda, calling for a conceptual shift away from understanding child abuse as what happens to younger children within the home and extending it to encompass the complex ways in which adolescents may be exploited and abused.

In addition to this, our research shows that practitioners need better awareness and understanding of the various forms that trafficking can take and of the way that trafficking becomes embedded in a young person's trajectory. It may take a long time to be disclosed and addressed. Training is needed to focus on the indicators of trafficking, the different reasons why young people are trafficked, the changing dynamics between international and internal trafficking, the way that each of these inform our understanding of 'childhood' and of 'home', and the length of time that it may take to both identify and address the significant harm caused by the experience of being trafficked.

For any service or relationship with a carer to be understood, the young person needs to be able to communicate in a shared language. Our research shows that the use of generically trained interpreters is not sufficient for work with trafficked young people. Specialist interpreters are needed who have undergone training on the forms and nature of trafficking and on understanding dynamics occurring for adolescents during their transition to adulthood.

Service provision

Our data clearly identify some specific developments that need to take place in service development to meet the needs of trafficked young people.

Our work supports that of other agencies who have noted that intrusive methods of assessing the young person's age at their point of entry to the country are abusive. Instead, age assessment should, if it is necessary, take place over a longer period of time once the young person is more confident and settled in accommodation.

It may never be possible to gather the exact age of a young person and this should be understood as disturbing for the young person concerned rather than for those trying to ascertain whether the young person has rights to remain in the country. Not to know how old you are is a denial of one of the significant indicators of identity and status. The need for age assessment should be driven by concern for the welfare of the child, rather than by immigration concerns and should take place over time while the young person is in a supportive and safe environment.

Once identified, young people should be provided with safe accommodation rather than ever being placed in bed and breakfast or hostel accommodation. Providing safe accommodation means developing a system of support around trained foster carer or residential care workers. This includes giving them immediate access to a named police officer, to a statutory key worker with care plan responsibilities and, if possible, to a project offering detached youth work that can engage in outreach work on the street.

It was clear from the research that education services play a pivotal role in helping the young person to settle and engage with their new community and that individual schools need support and resources to affect this process. Schools supported by school nurses and on-site language support systems provided well for trafficked young people. It was apparent from the work that, wherever possible, integration into the school rather than location in off-site provision was beneficial to the young person. However, this does not happen in isolation and the school needs additional resources to enable such services to work effectively and to liaise with other services engaged in the multi-agency framework delivering the care plan.

Similarly, members of health services, including sexual and mental health services, need training in indicators of trafficking, resources and enforced procedures for information sharing so that intelligence can be used as evidence to prosecute alleged abusers.

In essence, a reoccurring theme throughout the book has been that no one agency can respond to and meet the needs of trafficked young people on their own. As responses need to engage with the holistic nature of the young person's well-being, agencies need to share information about the different aspects of young people's needs and consult together on future planning to safeguard the young person. This means child protection services working in genuinely collaborative multidisciplinary teams, ideally co-located and addressing the dual purpose of safeguarding the young person while building intelligence that can be used to prosecute traffickers.

Summary

Calling for resources and improved training raises tensions in times of austerity and cutbacks in services and when competing demands are positioned against each other for attention. Recent media coverage of the horrific abuse experienced by some sexually exploited young people has raised the profile of trafficked young people, helping to engage practitioners and policy makers in discussions about how best to safeguard young people. Some of the media coverage of these prosecutions has placed particular focus on the gender and ethnicity of abuser and abused. Rather than expand awareness of these issues, this coverage has limited our understanding, reducing awareness of sexual exploitation and trafficking to that of white young female 'victims' and minority ethic ' perpetrators'. Our research has shown that society overall and many practitioners in particular have a poor representation or understanding of the full range of the experiences of trafficked young people.

This research calls for a sophisticated, informed and developed understanding of the range of issues facing all trafficked young people. It calls for the welfare of the child to override any immigration questions and for a multi-agency response to their needs to facilitate safe accommodation and access to basic health and education services. Identifying the social construction of both 'childhood' and 'home', the research has shown how the young person's experience is located in their transition to adulthood, effected by supported integration into mainstream services and into autonomous, informed and self-determined futures.

Indeed, without colluding with limited concepts of 'normality', it is pertinent for us to quote a young person at this point, who exclaimed to their practitioner that they 'just wanted to be normal!' By that, they were expressing a desire to leave behind their experience of having been trafficked, to move on and to take advantage of the opportunities that life offers in the way that any other young person can be expected to do. This, in essence, is what the United Nations Convention on the Rights of the Child is all about. We have argued throughout this book that by placing the trafficking of children first and foremost as a child protection issue in a collaborative multi-agency context with trained and supported practitioners we can help to enable exploited and abused young people to achieve these basic ambitions.

Appendix of tables

Table 1 The numbers of practitioners attending focus groups in each of the three sites and the numbers of trafficked children and young people (TCYP) they had worked with

Site	Number of practitioners	Worked with 0 TCYP	Worked with fewer than 5 TCYP	Worked with 5–10 TCYP	Worked with 10–20 TCYP	Worked with more than 20 TCYP
Site 1	23	1	6	3	2	11
Site 2	17	4	3	4	4	2
Site 3	25	16	4	2		3
Total	65	21	13	9	6	16

Table 2 The professional status of practitioners in focus groups (FG) and interviews

Agency or profession	Site 1 FG	Site 2 FG	Site 3 FG	Total in FG	Attending interviews but not FG
Young persons' drug and alcohol worker	0	0	1	1	
Health worker					
GP and hospital based health workers	0	1	1	2	
Looked-after children's nurses	3	4	0	7	
Education welfare and school-based education support workers	2	2	2	6	1
Social workers, including Local Safeguarding Children Board	6	5	7	18	2
Independent reviewing officer	2	1	0	2	
Children's centre support worker	1	1	1	3	
Children's residential worker	3	2	1	7	
Asylum team worker	2	0	1	3	
Police	1	0	3	4	3
UK Border Agency	1	0	0	1	
NGO provision for children and young people	2	0	7	9	
Crown Prosecution Service	0	0	1	1	
Youth Offending Team	0	1	0	1	1
Total	**23**	**17**	**25**	**65**	**7**

Table 3 Number and types of case studies analysed

Site	Cases of trafficking into UK from abroad	Cases of trafficking of UK citizens	Total cases of trafficking analysed
1	16		16
2	10	4	14
3	1	6	7
Total	27	10	37

NB: the 37 cases included 18 cases of the child having been reported missing

Table 4 Gender and age of trafficked children in the 37 case studies analysed

Age	Girls				Boys				Gender unknown				Total
	Female UK citizens trafficked		Girls trafficked into the UK from abroad		Male UK citizens trafficked abroad		Boys trafficked into the UK from abroad		UK citizens trafficked		Children and young people trafficked into UK from abroad		
	Sexual exploitation	Other	Sexual exploitation	Other	Sexual exploitation	Other	Sexual exploitation	Other	Sexual exploitation	Other	Sexual exploitation	Other	
3 and under	0	0	0	2	0	0	0	1	0	0	0	3	6
4–8	0	0	0	1	0	0	0	0	0	0	0	0	1
9–12	0	0	0	1	0	0	0	0	0	0	0	0	1
13–15	5	0	6	3	0	0	0	1	0	0	0	0	15
16 and 17	4	0	3	5	0	1	1	0	0	0	0	0	14
Totals	9	0	9	12	0	1	1	2	0	0	0	3	37

Table 5 Reasons for trafficking in the 37 case studies analysed

Sexual exploitation	Forced marriage	Domestic servitude	Benefit fraud/ illegal adoption	Restaurant work	Drug trafficking	Not known	Total
19	2	5	7	2	1	1	37

Table 6 Country of origin of the children and young people in the 37 cases studied

UK	10
China	8
Nigeria	8
Somalia	1
Pakistan	1
Cameroon	1
Ghana	1
Congo	1
Sierra Leone	1
Zimbabwe	1
Uganda	1
Vietnam	1
Eastern European country	1
Unknown	1
Total	37

Bibliography

Agustin, L. (2008) *Sex at the Margins: Migration, Labour Markets and the Rescue Industry.* London: Zed Books.

Allnock, D. (2010) 'Children and Young People Disclosing Sexual Abuse: An Introduction to the Research', NSPCC Research Briefing, London.

Allnock, D. and Hynes, P. (2011) *Therapeutic Services for Sexually Abused Children and Young People: Scoping the Evidence Base.* London: NSPCC.

Anderson, B. (2007) 'A Very Private Business: Exploring the Demand for Migrant Domestic Workers', *European Journal of Women's Studies,* 14(3):247–264.

Anderson, B. and O'Connell Davidson, J. (2004) *Trafficking: A Demand Led Problem? Part I: A Review of Evidence and Debates.* Stockholm: Save the Children.

Anti-Trafficking Monitoring Group (2010) *Wrong Kind of Victim? One Year On: An Analysis of UK Measures to Protect Trafficked Persons.* London: Anti-Trafficking Monitoring Group.

Anti-Trafficking Monitoring Group (2012) *All Change: Preventing Human Trafficking in the UK.* London: Anti-Slavery International for Anti-Trafficking Monitoring Group.

Asmussen, K. (2010) 'Key Facts about Child Maltreatment', NSPCC Research Briefing, London.

Ayer, P. and Preston-Shoot, M. (eds) (2010) *Children's Services at the Crossroads: A Critical Evaluation of Contemporary Policy for Practice.* Lyme Regis: Russell House.

Aynsley-Green, A. (2007) 'Does Every Unaccompanied Child Matter?', paper presented at conference, A Safer Future for Unaccompanied Children: The Challenge for Local Authorities in Implementing the UASC Reform Programme, London, 5 July.

BAAF (British Association for Adoption and Fostering) (2012) 'Statistics: England', at www.baaf.org.uk/res/statengland (accessed Sept. 2012).

Beck, U. (1992) *Risk Society: Towards a New Modernity.* London: Sage.

Beddoe, C. (2007) *Missing Out: A Study of Child Trafficking in the North-West, North-East and West Midlands.* London: ECPAT UK.

Bernard, C. and Gupta, A. (2006) 'Black African Children and the Child Protection System', *British Journal of Social Work,* 38(3):476–92.

Bloch, A. and Schuster, L. (2005) 'At the Extremes of Exclusion: Deportation, Detention and Dispersal', *Ethnic and Racial Studies*, 28(3): 491–512.

Bokhari, F. (2008) 'Falling through the Gaps: Safeguarding Children Trafficked into the UK', *Children and Society*, 22(3): 201–11

Bokhari, F. (2009) *Stolen Futures: Trafficking for Forced Child Marriage in the UK*. London: ECPAT UK and Wilberforce Institute for the Study of Slavery and Emancipation.

Bovarnick, S. (2010) 'How Do You Define a "Trafficked Child"? A Discursive Analysis of Practitioners' Perceptions around Child Trafficking',*Youth and Policy*, no.104 (June): 80–96.

Boyden, J. and Hart, J. (2007) 'Editorial Introduction: The Statelessness of the World's Children', *Children and Society*, 21(4): 237–48.

Breuil, B.C.O. (2008) '"Precious Children in a Heartless World"? The Complexities of Child Trafficking in Marseille', *Children and Society*, 22(3): 223–34.

Brodie, I., Melrose, M., Pearce, J. J. and Warrington, C. (2011) *Providing Safe and Supported Accommodation for Young People Who Are in the Care System and Who Are at Risk of, or Experiencing, Sexual Exploitation or Trafficking for Sexual Exploitation*. London: NSPCC.

Buck, T. and Nicholson, A. (2010) 'Constructing the International Legal Framework', in G. Craig (ed.), *Child Slavery Now: A Contemporary Reader*, Bristol: Policy Press.

Burgoyne, B. (2011) 'How Can We Make Multi-Agency Work in the Area of Child Trafficking More Effective', Children's Workforce Development Council, practitioner-led research programme, 2008–9, at http://dera.ioe.ac.uk/2775/ (accessed Sept. 2012).

Castles, S. (2002) 'Towards a Sociology of Forced Migration and Social Transformation', *Sociology*, 37(2): 12–34.

Castles, S. and Davidson, A. (2000) *Citizenship and Migration: Globalization and the Politics of Belonging*. New York: Routledge.

Cawson, P., Wattam, C., Brooker, S. and Kelly, G. (2000) *Child Maltreatment in the United Kingdom: A Study of the Prevalence of Child Abuse and Neglect.* London: NSPCC.

CEOP (Child Exploitation and Online Protection) (2007) *A Scoping Project on Child Trafficking in the UK*. London: CEOP.

CEOP (Child Exploitation and Online Protection) (2009) *Strategic Threat Assessment: Child Trafficking in the UK*. London: CEOP.

CEOP (Child Exploitation and Online Protection) (2011) *Out of Mind, Out of Sight: Breaking Down the Barriers to Understanding Child Sexual Exploitation.* London: CEOP.

CEOP (Child Exploitation and Online Protection), NSPCC CTAIL (Child Trafficking Advice and Information Line) and UKHTC (UK Human Trafficking Centre) (2011) 'Child Trafficking Update', CEOP, London.

Chandran, P. (2011) 'The Rights of Children Trafficked into the UK', Office of the Children's Commissioner for England, London.

Chase, E., Knight, A. and Statham, J. (2008) 'Promoting the Emotional Wellbeing and Mental Health of Unaccompanied Young People Seeking Asylum in the

UK (Research Summary)', Thomas Coram Research Unit, Institute of Education, London.

Coleman, J. (2011) *The Nature of Adolescence.* London: Routledge.

Coleman, J. and Hagel, A. (2007) *Adolescence, Risk and Resilience: Against the Odds.*Chichester: John Wiley & Sons.

Cook, B. (2009) 'Teenagers Need Safeguarding Too', *Children and Young People Now* (3–9 Dec.).

Cooper, A. and Lousada, J. (2005) *Borderline: Feeling and Fear of Feeling in Modern Welfare.* London: Karnac.

Craig, G. (2008) 'Editorial Introduction', *Children and Society*, 22(3):147–9.

Craig, G. (ed.) (2010) *Child Slavery Now: A Contemporary Reader.* Bristol: Policy Press.

Craig, G., Gaus, A., Wilkinson, M., Skrivankova, K. and McQuade, A. (2007) *Contemporary Slavery in the UK: Overview and Key Issues.* York: Joseph Rowntree Foundation.

Crawley, H. (2006) *Child First, Migrant Second: Ensuring that Every Child Matters.* London: Immigration Law Practitioners Association.

Crawley, H. (2007) *When Is a Child Not a Child? Asylum, Age Disputes and the Process of Age Assessment.* London: Immigration Law Practitioners' Association.

DCSF (Department for Children, Schools and Families) (2006) *Working Together to Safeguard Children.* London: HMSO.

DCSF (Department for Children, Schools and Families) (2007) *Safeguarding Children Who May Have Been Trafficked.* London: HMSO.

DCSF (Department for Children, Schools and Families) (2008a) *Staying Safe Action Plan.* London: HMSO.

DCSF (Department for Children, Schools and Families) (2008b) 'UK Lifts Reservations on the UN Convention on the Rights of the Child', press notice, 22 Sept., at http://webarchive.nationalarchives.gov.uk/20080929160223/http://dcsf.gov.uk/pns/DisplayPN.cgi?pn_id=2008_0209 (accessed Sept. 2012).

Department for Education (2011) 'Children Looked After by Local Authorities in England (including Adoption and Care Leavers): Year Ending 31 March 2011', Statistical First Release, at http://www.education.gov.uk/rsgateway/DB/SFR/s001026/index.shtml (accessed Sept. 2012).

Doezema, J. (2010) *Sex Slaves and Discourse Masters: The Construction of Trafficking.* London: Zed Books.

Dotteridge, M. (2004) *Kids as Commodities? Child Trafficking and What to Do about It.* Lausanne: Terre des Hommes.

Dowling, S., Moreton, K. and Wright, L. (2007) *Trafficking for the Purposes of Labour Exploitation: A Literature Review*, Home Office Online Report 10/07. London: Home Office.

Dwyer, P., Lewis, H., Scullion, L. and Waite, L. (2011) *Forced Labour and UK Immigration Policy: Status Matters?* York: Joseph Rowntree Foundation.

ECPAT UK (End Child Prostitution, Child Pornography and Trafficking of Children for Sexual Purposes UK) (2007) *Missing Out: A Study of Child Trafficking in the North-West, North-East and West Midlands.* London: ECPAT UK.

ECPAT UK (End Child Prostitution, Child Pornography and Trafficking of Children for Sexual Purposes UK) (2009a) *Bordering on Concern: Child Trafficking in Wales/ FfiniauPryder: Masnachu Plant yngNghymru.* London: ECPAT UK and Children's Commissioner for Wales.

ECPAT UK (End Child Prostitution, Child Pornography and Trafficking of Children for Sexual Purposes UK) (2009b) *Stolen Futures: Trafficking for Forced Child Marriage in the UK.* London: ECPAT UK.

ECPAT UK (End Child Prostitution, Child Pornography and Trafficking of Children for Sexual PurposesUK) (2010) *Safeguarding Children Trafficked to the UK to Undertake Forced Labour in Cannabis Factories.* London: ECPAT UK.

ECPAT UK (End Child Prostitution, Child Pornography and Trafficking of Children for Sexual Purposes UK) (2011a) *On the Safe Side: Principles for the Safe Accommodation of Child Victims of Trafficking.* London: ECPAT UK.

ECPAT UK (End Child Prostitution, Child Pornography and Trafficking of Children for Sexual Purposes UK) (2011b) *Watch over Me: A System of Guardianship for Child Victims of Trafficking.* London: ECPAT UK.

Every, D. and Augoustinos, M. (2007) 'Constructions of Racism in the Australian Parliamentary Debates on Asylum Seekers', *Discourse and Society*, 18(4): 411–36. DOI: 10.1177/0957926507077427.

Firmin, C. (2010) *The Female Voice in Violence.* London: Race on the Agenda (ROTA).

Fursland, E. (2009) *Caring for a Young Person Who Has Been Trafficked: A Guide for Foster Carers.* London: British Association for Adoption and Fostering (BAAF).

Gamble, J. (2008) *Children Are Not Commodities: Child Trafficking Is Child Abuse.* London: CEOP.

Garrett, P.M. (2006) 'Protecting Children in a Globalized World: "Race" and "Place" in the Laming Report on the Death of Victoria Climbié', *Journal of Social Work*, 6(3): 315–36.

Harris, J. and Robinson, B. (2007) *Tipping the Iceberg: A Pan Sussex Study of Young People at Risk of Sexual Exploitation and Trafficking – Final Report.* Barkingside: Barnardo's.

Hart, J. and Tyrer, B. (2006) *Research with Children Living in Situations of Armed Conflict: Concepts, Ethics and Methods*, Working Paper Series No.30. Oxford: Refugee Studies Centre.

Herzfeld, B., Green, S., Epstein, S. and Beddoe, C. (2006) 'Trafficking: Immigration or Human Rights Concern?', *Forced Migration Review*, 25:39–40.

Hicks, L. and Stein, M. (2010) *Neglect Matters: A Multi-Agency Guide for Professionals Working Together on Behalf of Teenagers.* London: Department for Children, Schools and Families. At https://www.education.gov.uk/publications/standard/Integratedworking/Page1/DCSF-00247-2010 (accessed Sept. 2012).

Home Office (2008a) 'Supplementary Tables for 2008, including Applications Received for Asylum in the UK from Unaccompanied Children', Home Office, London.

Home Office (2008b) *Update to the UK Action Plan on Tackling Human Trafficking.* London: HMSO.

Home Office (2010) 'Migration Statistics', at http://www.homeoffice.gov.uk/sci-ence-research/research-statistics/migration/migration-statistics1/ (accessed Oct. 2012).

Home Office (2011) *Human Trafficking: The Government's Strategy*. At http://www. homeoffice.gov.uk/publications/crime/human-trafficking-strategy (accessed Sept. 2012).

Howe, D. (1998) 'Relationship-Based Thinking and Practice in Social Work', *Journal of Social Work Practice*, special issue, 12(1): 45–56.

Hughes, L. and Owen, H. (2009) *Good Practice in Safeguarding Children: Working Effectively in Child Protection*. London: Jessica Kingsley.

Hynes, P. (2007) 'Dispersal of Asylum Seekers and Processes of Social Exclusion in England', Ph.D. thesis, Middlesex University.

Hynes, P. (2009) 'Contemporary Compulsory Dispersal and the Absence of Space for the Restoration of Trust', *Journal of Refugee Studies*, 22(1):97–121.

Hynes, P. (2010a) 'Global Points of "Vulnerability": Understanding Processes of the Trafficking of Children and Young People into, within and out of the UK', *International Journal of Human Rights*, 14(6):952–70.

Hynes, P. (2010b) 'Understanding the "Vulnerabilities", "Resilience" and Processes of the Trafficking of Children and Young People into, within and out of the UK', *Youth and Policy*, no. 104 (June): 97–118.

Hynes, P., Lamb, M., Short, D. and Waites, M. (eds) (2011) *Sociology and Human Rights*. London: Routledge.

Hynes, T. (2003) 'The Issue of "Trust" or "Mistrust" in Research with Refugees: Choices, Caveats and Considerations for Researchers', Working Paper No. 98, Evaluation and Policy Analysis Unit, United Nations High Commission for Refugees, Geneva.

Itzin, C., Taket, A. and Barter-Godfrey, S. (2010) *Domestic and Sexual Violence and Abuse: Tackling the Health and Mental Health Effects*. London: Routledge.

Jago, S. and Pearce, J. (2008) 'Gathering Evidence of the Sexual Exploitation of Children and Young People: A Scoping Exercise', University of Bedfordshire, Luton.

Jago, S., Arocha, L., Brodie, I., Melrose, M., Pearce, J. and Warrington, C. (2011) 'What's Going On to Safeguard Children and Young People from Sexual Exploitation?', University of Bedfordshire, Luton.

James, A. and Prout, A. (1997) *Constructing and Reconstructing Childhood: Contemporary Issues in the Sociological Study of Childhood*. London: Falmer Press.

James, A., Jenks, C. and Prout, A. (1996) *Theorizing Childhood*. Cambridge: Polity.

Jobe, A. (2008) 'A New Sexual Story: Trafficking, Immigration and Asylum – the Converging of Discourses', in F. Alexander and K. Throsby (eds), *Gender and Interpersonal Violence: Language, Action and Representation*, Basingstoke: Palgrave Macmillan.

Jobe, A. (2010) 'Accessing Help and Services: Trafficking Survivors' Experiences in the United Kingdom', in P. McRedmond and G. Wylie (eds), *Human Trafficking in Europe: Character, Causes and Consequences*, Basingstoke: Palgrave Macmillan, pp. 164–80.

Joint Committe on Human Rights (2007) *Tenth Report*. London: House of Lords and House of Commons.

Kelly, E. and Bokhari, F. (2011) *Safeguarding Children from Abroad: Refugee, Asylum Seeking and Trafficked Children in the UK*. London: Jessica Kingsley.

Kelly, L. (2005) "You Can Find Anything You Want": A Critical Reflection on Research on Trafficking in Persons within and into Europe', *International Migration*, special issue, 43(1/2):235–65.

King, R., Skeldon, R. and Vullnetari, J. (2008) 'Internal and International Migration: Bridging the Theoretical Divide', Working Paper 52, Sussex Centre for Migration Research, University of Sussex.

Kohli, R.K.S. and Mitchell, F. (eds) (2007) *Working with Unaccompanied Asylum Seeking Children: Issues for Policy and Practice*. Basingstoke: Palgrave Macmillan.

Korbin, J.E. (2007) 'Issues of Culture', in K. Wilson and A. James (eds), *The Child Protection Handbook*. Edinburgh: Baillière Tindall,

Kunz, E.F. (1973) 'The Refugee in Flight: Kinetic Models and Forms of Displacement', *International Migration Review*, 7(2):125–46.

Laming, Lord (2003) *The Victoria Climbié Inquiry: Report of an Inquiry by Lord Laming*. Cm 5730. Norwich: HMSO.

Laming, Lord (2009) *The Protection of Children in England: A Progress Report*. London: HMSO.

Lillywhite, R. and Skidmore, P. (2006) 'Boys Are Not Sexually Exploited? A Challenge to Practitioners', *Child Abuse Review*, 15(5): 351–61.

London Safeguarding Children Board (2011) *London Safeguarding Trafficked Children Toolkit*. London: London Safeguarding Children Board. Piloted 2009.

Luthar, S. (ed.) (2003) *Resilience and Vulnerability*. Cambridge: Cambridge University Press.

Luxmoore, N. (2008) *Feeling like Crap: Young People and the Meaning of Self Esteem*. London: Jessica Kingsley.

Mann, G. (2001) *Networks of Support: A Literature Review of Care Issues for Separated Children*, London: Save the Children.

Marie, A. and Skidmore, P. (2007) *A Summary Report Mapping the Scale of Internal Trafficking in the UK Based on a Survey of Barnardo's Anti-Sexual Exploitation and Missing Services*. Ilford: Barnardo's.

Meetoo, V. and Mirza, H. (2007) '"There's Nothing 'Honourable' about Honour Killings": Gender, Violence and the Limits of Multiculturalism', *Women's Studies International Forum*, 30(3): 187–200.

Melrose, M. (2010) 'What's Love Got to Do with It? Theorising Young People's Involvement in Prostitution', *Youth and Policy*, no. 104 (June): 12–30.

Melrose, M. (2011) 'Regulating Social Research: Exploring the Implications of Extending Ethical Review Processes in Social Research', *Sociological Research Online*, 36(2), at www.socresonline.org.uk/16/2/14.html (accessed Sept. 2012).

Morrison, J. (2000) *The Trafficking and Smuggling of Refugees: The End Game in European Asylum Policy?* Geneva: United Nations High Commissioner for Refugees.

Morrison, J. (2002) 'Human Smuggling and Trafficking', Forced Migration

Online guide, at http://www.forcedmigration.org/research-resources/expert-guides/human-smuggling-and-trafficking (accessed Sept. 2012).

Mullenger, N. (2000) 'Immigrants and Illegal Youth Sex Workers in Italy', in D. Barrett, E. Barrett and N. Mullenger (eds), *Youth Prostitution in the New Europe: The Growth in Sex Work.* Lyme Regis: Russell House.

Munro, E. (2011) *The Munro Review of Child Protection: Final Report. A Child-Centred System.* London: HMSO.

O'Connell Davidson, J. (2005) *Children in the Global Sex Trade.* Cambridge: Polity.

O'Connell Davidson, J. and Farrow, C. (2007) *Child Migration and the Construction of Vulnerability.* Stockholm: Save the Children.

OHCHR (Office of the High Commissioner for Human Rights) (2012) 'Migration and Human Rights', at http://www.ohchr.org/EN/Issues/Migration/Pages/Migration And HumanRightsIndex.aspx (accessed Oct. 2012).

Oliver, M. (1990) *The Politics of Disablement.* Basingstoke: Macmillan.

Operation Pentameter (2006) 'Operational Overview', at www.cps.gov.uk/publications/docs/pentameter_0706.pdf (accessed Oct. 2012).

Owen, C. and Statham, J. (2009) *Disproportionality in Child Welfare: The Prevalence of Black and Minority Ethnic Children within the 'Looked After' and 'Children in Need' Populations and on Child Protection Registers in England.* London: Department for Children, Schools and Families and Thomas Coram Research Unit, Institute of Education, University of London.

Papadopoulos, L. (2010) *The Sexualisation of Young People: Review.* London: Department of Health.

Parton, N. (2011) 'Child Protection and Safeguarding in England: Changing and Competing Conceptions of Risk and their Implications for Social Work', *British Journal of Social Work*, 41:854–75.

Pearce, J.J. (2007) 'Sex and Risk', in J. Coleman and A. Hagell (eds), *Adolescence, Risk and Resilience: Against the Odds*, Chichester: John Wiley & Sons.

Pearce, J.J. (2009) *Young People and Sexual Exploitation: It Isn't Hidden, You Just Aren't Looking.* London: Routledge.

Pearce, J. J. (2010) 'Safeguarding Young People from Sexual Exploitation and from being Trafficked: Tensions within Contemporary Policy and Practice', *Youth and Policy*, no. 104 (June), special issue.

Pearce, J.J. (2011) 'Working with Trafficked Children and Young People: Complexities in Practice', *British Journal of Social Work* 41(8): 1424–41.

Pearce, J. (forthcoming) 'Contextualising "Consent" in Child Sexual Exploitation', in M. Melrose and J. Pearce (eds), *Critical Perspectives on Child Sexual Exploitation*, Basingstoke: Palgrave Macmillan.

Pearce, J. and Pitts, J. (2011) *Sexual Violence and Sexual Exploitation in Gang Affected Neighbourhoods.* Luton: University of Bedfordshire.

Pearce, J. J., Hynes, P. and Bovarnick, S. (2009) *Breaking the Wall of Silence: Practitioners' Responses to Trafficked Children and Young People.* London: NSPCC.

Philips, M. (2007) 'Issues of Ethnicity', in K. Wilson and A. James (eds), *The Child Protection Handbook*, Edinburgh: Baillière Tindall.

Pitts, J. (2008) *Reluctant Gangsters: The Changing Face of Youth Crime.* Cullompton: Willan.

Reale, D. (2008) *Away from Home: Protecting and Support Children on the Move.* London: Save the Children.

Rees, G., Gorin, S., Jobe, A., Stein, M., Medforth, R. and Goswami, H. (2010) *Safeguarding Young People: Responding to Young People Aged 11 to 17 Who Are Maltreated.* London: Children's Society.

Rees, G., Stein, M., Hicks, L. and Gorin, S. (2011) *Adolescent Neglect: Research, Policy and Practice.* London: Jessica Kingsley.

Richmond, A.H. (1994) *Global Apartheid: Refugees, Racism and the New World Order.* Oxford: Oxford University Press.

Sales, R. (2007) *Understanding Immigration and Refugee Policy; Contradictions and Continuities.* London: Policy Press.

Salt, J. (2000) 'Trafficking and Human Smuggling: A European Perspective', *International Migration*, special issue, 38(3): 31–56.

Scott, S. and Skidmore, P. (2006) *Reducing the Risk: Barnardo's Support for Sexually Exploited Young People: A Two Year Evaluation.* Ilford: Barnardo's.

Separated Children in Europe Programme (2009) *Statement of Good Practice*, 4th rev.edn. At http://www.unhcr.org/refworld/pdfid/415450694.pdf(accessed Sept. 2012).

Separated Children in Europe Programme and Save the Children (2007) *Position Paper on Preventing and Responding to Trafficking of Children in Europe.* London: International Save the Children Alliance.

Shakespeare, T. and Watson, N. (2002) 'The Social Model of Disability: An Outdated Ideology?', *Research in Social Science and Disability*, 2: 9–28.

Sigona, N. and Hughes, V. (2010) 'Being Children and Undocumented: A Background Paper', COMPAS Working Paper 78–10, Oxford.

Sillen, J. and Beddoe, C. (2007) *Rights Here, Rights Now: Recommendations for Protecting Trafficked Children.* London: ECPAT and UNICEF.

Skrivankova, K. (2010) *Between Decent Work and Forced Labour: Examining the Continuum of Exploitation.* York: Joseph Rowntree Foundation.

Solomos, J. (2003) *Race and Racism in Britain.* Basingstoke: Palgrave Macmillan.

Somerset, C. (2004) *Cause for Concern? London Social Services and Child Trafficking.* London: ECPAT.

Taskforce on the Health Aspects of Violence against Women and Children (2010) 'Report from the Sexual Violence against Women Sub-group: Responding to Violence against Women and Children – the Role of the NHS', Department of Health, London.

United Nations (2000) *Protocol against the Smuggling of Migrants by Land, Sea and Air, Supplementing the United Nations Convention against Transnational Organized Crime.* New York: United Nations.

UNODC (United Nations Office on Drugs and Crime) (2000) *Protocol to Prevent, Suppress and Punish Trafficking in Persons, especially Women and Children, supplementing the United Nations Convention against Transnational Organized Crime* (Palermo Protocol). At http://www.unodc.org/unodc/en/treaties/CTOC/index.html (accessed Sept. 2012).

van de Glind, H. (2010) 'Child Trafficking: A Modern Form of Slavery', in G. Craig (ed.), *Child Slavery Now: A Contemporary Reader*, Bristol: Policy Press.

Wood, Marsha, Barter, Christine and Berridge, David (2011) *Standing on My Own Two Feet: Disadvantaged Teenagers, Intimate Partner Violence and Coercive Control*. London: NSPCC, 2011.

Zetter, R., Griffiths, D., Ferretti, S. and Pearl, M. (2003) *An Assessment of the Impact of Asylum Policies in Europe 1990–2000*, Research Study 259. London: Home Office.

Zimmerman, C. and Watts, C. (2003) *WHO Ethical and Safety Recommendations for Interviewing Trafficked Women*. Geneva: World Health Organization.

Zimmerman, C., Hossain, M. and Yun, K. (2006) *Stolen Smiles: A Summary Report on the Physical and Psychological Health Consequences of Women and Adolescents Trafficked in Europe*. London: London School of Hygiene and Tropical Medicine.

Index